FACT,
FICTION,
AND POLYGAMY

HENRIETTA POLYDORE (1846–1874),
HEROINE OF BROWNE'S NOVELLA

Undated photo of Henrietta, probably taken by William Jeffrey, a prominent British photographer specializing in creating albumen carte-de-visite images during the mid-1860s. *Courtesy of Victoria and Albert Museum, London.*

FACT, FICTION, AND POLYGAMY

A TALE OF UTAH WAR INTRIGUE
1857–1858

A. G. Browne's *The Ward of the Three Guardians*

EDITED BY
WILLIAM P. MACKINNON AND
KENNETH L. ALFORD

FOREWORD BY RICHARD E. TURLEY JR.

NUMBER SEVENTEEN IN THE SERIES
UTAH, THE MORMONS, AND THE WEST
Tanner Trust Fund and J. Willard Marriott Library

Fact, Fiction, and Polygamy—A Tale of Utah War Intrigue, 1857–1858:
A.G. Browne's *The Ward of the Three Guardians*

ISBN 978-1-64769-069-4
LCCN 2021952173

For
PATRICIA H. MACKINNON
With gratitude for her love and wisdom.

For
SHERILEE B. ALFORD
More than yesterday; less than tomorrow.

Table of Contents

Illustrations

The present essay . . . explores the intricate relationship between western history and western fiction within the intimate circumference of micro-history. . . . Then, having perceived the interaction of fact and fiction at several points, the authors, in effect, turn conventional post-modern criticism on its head by examining a literary artifact as a historical text. They hypothesize that the novel supplies an important detail strangely missing from the historical record.

DYKSTRA AND MANFRA, "THE CIRCLE DOT COWBOYS
AT DODGE CITY: HISTORY AND IMAGINATION IN
ANDY ADAMS'S *THE LOG OF A COWBOY*," 2002

Foreword

THERE COMES A TIME IN THE PROFESSIONAL LIFE of most historians when, after years of research and hunting, they begin to feel that the primary sources of their areas of focus have largely been discovered, with little new remaining to find. I have felt that way from time to time in my decades-long search for the truth behind the Utah War's Mountain Meadows Massacre of September 1857. Yet each time I reach the brink of that seductive conclusion, something new and surprising surfaces, usually serendipitously.

A prime example is the rediscovery of the Utah War source at the heart of this study, Albert G. Browne, Jr.'s novella, *The Ward of the Three Guardians*. Hiding in plain sight, as historian-editors William P. MacKinnon and Kenneth L. Alford phrase it, the novella is a document that sheds new light on a military campaign that was America's most extensive and expensive military venture during the turbulent period between the Mexican and Civil Wars.

With nearly a century of Utah War studies between them, these two scholars are ideally suited to have spotted *Ward*, recognized it as the gem it is, and positioned it for use by those of us seeking either a good tale of the American West or a primary source created by the only war insider who was also a professional writer. It would be gilding the lily to call Browne the Stephen Crane of the Utah War, but he might well qualify as its Ambrose Bierce.

What is there about this study that makes it worth reading? For me, the answer lies in its perspective and scope. Utah War historians have long known of Browne as the Boston Brahmin who published a marvelous, early history of the conflict in the *Atlantic Monthly* during 1859. What Alford and MacKinnon now bring to our attention is an awareness that Browne's writings also included a series of anonymously published war dispatches for the *New-York Tribune*, as well as the short non-fiction novel later based on these reports. Taken together, Browne's work provides insight into this unprecedented territorial-federal conflict and is unique in its depth, richness, and readability.

In the process, Browne unwittingly reminds us that the Utah War was not the all-male show historians have often portrayed. With the Utah Expedition quartered for the winter only 113 miles from Salt Lake City, tens of thousands of Latter-day Saint women and girls were virtually on the war's front lines. They behaved accordingly. Conversely, as historian Audrey Godfrey has discussed elsewhere, women were also present in the midst of the U.S. Army's Utah Expedition—as officers' wives or laundresses, perhaps as many as eighty of them. But through *Ward* we also realize the war's impact on a twelve-year-old English girl sequestered in a polygamous Salt Lake City household peopled by five sister wives and nearly twenty other children. She was a fugitive sought jointly by the British Crown and the U.S. government, a girl who was first cousin to the Rossetti siblings, two of England's most accomplished poets and painters of the mid-nineteenth century.

Within a mile of my home, Lot Smith—the Nauvoo Legion's most accomplished cavalryman—lies buried, oblivious in life that he frequently rode past the adobe harboring Henrietta Polydore under the alias "Lucy." Major Smith was not the only soldier oblivious to young Henrietta's presence there until Queen Victoria's foreign office and Gen. Albert Sidney Johnston came calling in Salt Lake City by force of arms.

Sit back and savor Albert Browne's newly recovered tale and its rich blend of fact and fantasy. With the guidance of editors MacKinnon and Alford, determining the difference is half the fun and much the value of revisiting *The Ward of the Three Guardians*.

Richard E. Turley Jr.
Former Assistant Historian and Recorder,
The Church of Jesus Christ of Latter-day Saints
Farmington, Utah

ALBERT GALLATIN BROWNE, JR. (1835–1891)
This undated photo, probably taken in the late 1860s or early 1870s, shows
Browne close to the time he wrote *Ward of the Three Guardians*. *Courtesy of
Browne family descendant Katherine Greenough.*

Acknowledgments

With an interest in Albert G. Browne, Jr. that goes back to 1958 and an awareness of his novella *The Ward of the Three Guardians* that first arose thirty years later, there are many individuals, families, and institutions who helped make this book possible. Among the most prominent of those encountered during this long editorial journey are the benefactors mentioned below.

Special thanks go to the late William Grant (Will) Bagley of Salt Lake City's Prairie Dog Press for ferreting out and sharing in 1998 a photocopy of the scrapbook in which Browne collected and annotated his *New-York Tribune* dispatches from the Utah War. It was this material, found in Special Collections of the University of Utah's J. Willard Marriott Library, that permitted us to confirm that Browne was indeed the author of these anonymous newspaper reports. The dispatch of August 5, 1858, in turn, was key to linking the identity of *Ward's* fictive "Henrietta Perego" and the actual Henrietta Polydore sequestered in Elder Samuel W. Richards' polygamous household during 1855–58. From Browne's annotations in this scrapbook also came confirmation that it was to nineteen-year-old David Auguste Burr that Browne entrusted responsibility for maintaining a stream of dispatches to the *New-York Tribune* while he trekked to the East from Fort Bridger and back during January–May 1858.

With this information in hand, we were then able to engage the considerable document-hunting talents of Utah historian-genealogist Ardis E. Parshall, who found primary sources about Browne and Polydore from the collections of a wide-ranging group of research libraries and historical societies. For a decades-long flow of such documents as well as her extraordinary transcription skills, we thank Ms. Parshall.

We gratefully acknowledge the editing, proofreading, layout, and artistic talents of Robert A. Clark and Ariane C. Smith, who are responsible for transforming our manuscript into this professionally finished book.

Descendants of the principal figures in this study have been especially generous in providing not only relevant documents and photographs but family folklore and insights about the people that have intrigued us as well as them. Among these is editor-author Maureen Carr Ward of Hyrum, Utah, a direct descendant of Samuel W. Richards and his first wife, one of Jane Mayer Richards' sister wives. Thanks also to several descendants of Judge Eckels, especially Robert Eckels of Arlington Heights, Illinois, and Larry M. Hutchinson of Gilbert, Arizona.

Especially helpful have been members of the extended Browne family located throughout the United States. Foremost among them has been the family's informal historian, Katherine Greenough of Boston, through whom we had access to the researcher's proverbial dream, an unexploited trunk in the attic. In this case the trove was tucked under the eaves of the Brownes' summer compound in Rockport, Massachusetts. With Ms. Greenough's thoughtful guidance, we also had the benefit of in-person meetings or email communications with several of her cousins, who, in turn, shared their documents, photographs, paintings, and recollections. Chief among these helpful family members are Charles B.

and Tina Browne, Robert Chamberlin, Steve Chamberlin, Mason Browne, Sally Chamberlin, and Louisa Soleau of Texas, North Carolina, Massachusetts, Virginia, California, and New York.

We are also grateful to the archivists, curators, and librarians at several institutions with collections bearing on our research. At Harvard University alone we are indebted to the staff of three libraries with holdings relating to Albert G. Browne. Over the decades, at Radcliffe Institute's Arthur and Elizabeth Schlesinger Library on the History of Women in America, a number of professionals helped us to access the Browne Family Papers, especially Jane Kamensky, director of the library; Elizabeth Shenton, assistant to the director; Ellen M. Shea, head of research services; Jane S. Knowles, archivist; and Giordana Mecagni, reference assistant. Michelle Gachette, reference assistant, enabled us to examine Harvard University's archives in Pusey Library and with them Browne's record and several photographs of him as a member of the Class of 1853. David Warrington, head of Special Collections for the Harvard Law School Library, led us to a photograph of a Civil War–era Albert not available elsewhere. We are also grateful to Ms. Jean Martin of *Harvard Magazine* for her help with graphic representations of Browne and in publishing in her journal a brief account of his experiences as a war correspondent in Utah.

In the Browne family's ancestral home of Salem, Massachusetts, we found a plethora of obituaries recording Albert's life and death in 1891. For this and other kindnesses, we thank Patrick J. Clotherty, director, and Christine Morin, reference librarian, at the Salem Public Library.

Thanks also to: Gregory C. Thompson, associate dean for special collections, J. Willard Marriott Library, University of Utah; George A. Miles, William Robertson Coe Curator of the Yale Collection of Western Americana, Beinecke Rare Book and

Manuscript Library, New Haven; Dorothy Hammond, Mary Wallace, and Tumara Marie Steinbach of the Pueblo, Colorado County Historical Society; Kellyn Youngren of the University of Montana's Mansfield Library in Missoula; Dr. Hans Ewald Kessler of Bavaria's Heidelberg University; and the staffs of Brigham Young University's Harold B. Lee Library, Provo and the Church History Library of The Church of Jesus Christ of Latter-day Saints, Salt Lake City. At the Research Center of Utah State Archives, Mr. Tony Castro was especially helpful in guiding us to the legal papers for the Polydore case adjudicated during August 1858 in Salt Lake City's U.S. district court, and, elsewhere in Salt Lake, we are indebted to Doug Meisner, library and collections coordinator at Utah State History, for images of several of the key players on whom this study focuses.

Aside from the staffs of these indispensable institutions, we are also indebted to several historians who have published insightful studies about various aspects of the society that surrounded Browne during his Boston years. Professor Albert J. von Frank of Washington State University's department of English was generous with his time and assessments of Browne's involvement in the 1854 Anthony Burns melee as well as his relationship with U.S. senator Charles Sumner. Richard F. Miller of Concord, Massachusetts, helped us to understand Browne's role seven years later as Governor Andrew's military secretary through personal communications as well as his multiple journal articles and books about the elite volunteer regiments that both men raised for service with the Union Army.

We appreciate the efforts of Natalie Packard, Deanna Nielson, Allison Thomson, Savannah Jardine, and Zachary Lambert—student research assistants at Brigham Young University who performed a variety of tasks that contributed to the final result—and

Beverly Yellowhorse, who so ably manages BYU's Religious Education Faculty Resource office, and her able student staff.

In the United Kingdom we owe thanks to several people who added to our understanding of the Henrietta Polydore aspects of the story. In London, independent researcher Elizabeth R. Talbot Rice guided us to the British diplomatic correspondence bearing on Henrietta's repatriation. In Gloucestershire, home to the Polydore and Mayer families, we are indebted to Helen Dorricott and Graham Baker of the Gloucestershire County Library, as well as to Sally Self of the Cheltenham Local History Society.

We also appreciate the willingness of Miles and Jill Butler of Devon, England, to share photographs and stories of their sailboat, *Henrietta Polydore*. This was not only a fortuitous, charming material connection to our subject but one that permitted part of our team (Alford) to relive his missionary days distributing tracts and seeking converts near the River Dart, current home port for the *Henrietta Polydore*. As the Butlers chart their course into the English Channel, the North Sea, and waters beyond, they now have not only the conventional aids to navigation by which to sail but the earlier adventures of Albert Browne and Christina Rossetti's "Lalla" to serve as inspiration.

Finally, we need to give thanks for the indispensable love and support of our spouses, Sherilee Alford of Springville, Utah, and Patricia H. MacKinnon of Montecito, California. Without their warmth, concern for our wellbeing, and good cheer over a sustained period of time, none of this would have been possible, and *Ward* would have continued to languish unappreciated. These ladies are neither our wards nor guardians, but we certainly are their grateful husbands.

In expressing our gratitude to these friends, benefactors, professional colleagues, and family members, we are mindful of one of our principal findings—that the geographical scope of the Utah War and Albert G. Browne's novella about it were indeed stories wide-ranging in their character and setting. We have unearthed and burnished them through the kindness of others as well as the unexpected blessing of serendipity. That has been the fun of it.

PART ONE

Understandings

There is no more striking instance of the way in which men of ability are "swallowed up and lost" in the large newspaper establishments than Albert G. Browne, of the New York *Herald*. A graduate of Harvard College, and a man of marked ability, Colonel Browne was the private secretary and most intimate friend of Gov. Andrew during his whole term of office. ... He and scores of able men like him have been absorbed in an establishment, which is the most remarkable in all time, and so completely lose their identity that when they die or are retired scarcely a ripple is created on the great stream, and their labors rest with them, as unknown in detail as the daily work of a London cab driver or a New York attorney.

EVERY OTHER SATURDAY—
A JOURNAL OF SELECT READING, NEW AND OLD
(BOSTON, FEBRUARY 2, 1884)

Editors' Introduction

BEFORE THE AMERICAN CIVIL WAR CAME THE
Utah War of 1857–58, the country's most extensive and
expensive military conflict since the Mexican-American War. By
its nature, the U.S. government's campaign to suppress what it
perceived to be a rebellion in Utah stimulated melodrama. American and European artists responded even while the war was in
progress. They created a plethora of plays, poems, novels, folk
songs, sheet music, and illustrations loaded with lurid accounts
of sex, massacres, heroics, and political hugger-mugger. It was
an outpouring that attempted to tell the war's story and fathom
its meaning through a cast of stereotypical characters including
polygamous patriarchs, damsels in distress, ecclesiastical assassins, defenders of the home hearth, corrupt federal appointees,
opportunistic contractors, military heroes, venal politicians,
enigmatic Indians, and stolid mountaineers.

Brigham Young's large extended family was especially creative
in writing about the Utah War. One of his wives and a son-in-law
each wrote verses as morale builders for Latter-day Saint troops,
couching their propaganda in anti-federal Yankee dialect. A
Brigham Young daughter composed a romantic novel involving a
Utah girl and a territorial militiaman, while a grandson, educated
at the U.S. Military Academy, published a non-fiction sketch of

the Nauvoo Legion that squared off against a U.S. Army expedition led by West Pointers.[1]

In Europe, a Prussian nobleman published a travelogue and series of James Fenimore Cooper–like novels based on his pioneering ascent of the Colorado River and its Grand Canyon to discover an invasion route into southern Utah.[2] A Boston poet composed a satire in mock-epic verse to lampoon polygamy as well as the wartime political foibles of both the Buchanan administration and Latter-day Saints.[3] Manhattan's impresarios staged plays about the war, some in Irish dialect. In September 1857 both the *New York Times* and the *New-York Tribune* ran a multipart potboiler with the indigestible title *Ardine; or, The Avenger*

---

1   Brigham Young's grandson, Richard Whitehead Young (USMA Class of 1882, Cullum #2946) wrote a year-long series about the Utah War titled "The Nauvoo Legion" [*The Contributor* 9, No. 1 (November 1887)—No. 12 (October 1888)]; Hiram B. Clawson, husband to two of Brigham Young's daughters and a brigadier general in the Nauvoo Legion, composed "Young Sam—A Yankee Story" in dialect and had it printed as a propaganda piece on November 9, 1857; rare copies may be found in the Hiram B. Clawson Papers, Church History Library, The Church of Jesus Christ of Latter-day Saints, Salt Lake City, and in Yale Collection of Western Americana, Beinecke Library, New Haven, Conn. Inspired by a public reading of Clawson's piece on December 4, 1857, Eliza Roxcy Snow (widow of Joseph Smith and wife of Brigham Young) composed lyrics titled "Young Sam and His Uncle" set to the music of Stephen Foster's popular "De Camptown Races;" Church History Library. See also Susa Young Gates, *John Stevens' Courtship: A Story of the Echo Canyon War* (Salt Lake City: Deseret News, 1909). Some material in this book has previously appeared in publications by the editors.

2   For an account of Heinrich Balduin Mollhausen's Utah War adventures on the Colorado River with the U.S. Army's Ives Expedition and the novels that followed, see Preston Albert Barba, *Balduin Mollhausen, the German* [James Fenimore] *Cooper* (Philadelphia: Publications of the University of Pennsylvania, *American Germanica* 17, 1914); David H. Miller, "The Ives Expedition Revisited: A Prussian's Impressions," *Journal of Arizona History* 13 (Spring 1972): 1–25; William P. MacKinnon, ed., "'A Channel of Communication with Utah': Rio Colorado," *At Sword's Point, Part 2: A Documentary History of the Utah War, 1858–1859* (Norman, Okla.: Arthur H. Clark, 2016), 113–41.

3   [Anonymous] *Mormoniad* (Boston: A. Williams & Co., 1858).

of Wrong: A Tale of Mormonism in New-York and the Far West; By a Fugitive.[4]

From this stew of overheated drama emerged the first of Arthur Conan Doyle's Sherlock Holmes stories, "A Study in Scarlet," that cast Latter-day Saints in a negative light.[5] In Bavaria, embezzler Karl May wrote wildly popular novels about Mormon villainy and frontier heroism in his prison cell, a series so captivating to an adolescent Adolph Hitler that he later distributed copies en mass to the Germany army. In the United States, novelists Robert Louis Stevenson and Zane Grey exploited Karl May's themes of Utah War violence and treachery for their own artistic purposes near the turn of the twentieth century.[6]

Except for the work of the Latter-day Saints involved, virtually none of this Utah War material was created by the conflict's participants, and few of the non-Latter-day Saint writers other than Doyle, Stevenson, and Grey ever ventured west of St. Louis. An exception to this pattern was *The Ward of the Three Guardians*, a novella written by Boston Brahmin Albert G. Browne, Jr. and published in *The Atlantic Monthly* during 1877.[7] Browne, the recipient of two Harvard degrees, a German Ph.D., and a homicide indictment, had worked in Utah twenty years earlier as a war reporter for Horace Greeley's *New-York Tribune*. In this civilian

---

4   *Ardine* ran in *New-York Tribune*, September 19, 1857, 1/3–5.

5   Arthur Conan Doyle, "A Study in Scarlet" in *Beeton's Christmas Annual* (London: Ward, Lock & Co., 1887), 1–95.

6   D. L. Ashliman, "The Image of Utah and the Mormons in Nineteenth-Century Germany," *Utah Historical Quarterly* 35 (Summer 1967): 209–27; Robert Louis Stevenson and Fanny van der Grift Stevenson, "Story of the Destroying Angel," in *More New Arabian Nights: The Dynamiter* (London: Longmans, Green & Co., 1885); Zane Grey, *Riders of the Purple Sage* (New York: Harper & Brothers, 1912).

7   As we are using the term, we consider a novella as a reasonably short work of fiction. Albert G. Browne, Jr., "The Ward of the Three Guardians," *The Atlantic Monthly* 39 (June 1877): 697–716.

role he accompanied the army expedition tasked with escorting Gov. Brigham Young's successor to Salt Lake City and restoring federal authority in the territory. What Browne wrote about Utah as both a reporter and novelist was a stand-out because he drew on his own first-hand observations, capitalized on unparalleled access to insider information, and published what he wrote in two of the great journals of the time.

The purpose of this study is to resurrect *The Ward of the Three Guardians* and present it in edited form relevant to a twenty-first-century readership. In the process, we will examine Browne's important role in a poorly understood military campaign while presenting, through his work, the even less familiar story of Henrietta Polydore. Here then is the twelve-year-old Anglo-Italian girl who inspired Browne with her dramatic flight from a Catholic convent school in England to sequestration in a Salt Lake City household with five wives, one of whom was her aunt.

In literary style, Browne's *Ward* was precursor to what American writer Truman Capote later dubbed the "non-fiction novel."[8] Henrietta's true story, as lightly fictionalized by Albert Browne, was an extraordinary tale. It is an adventure worth revisiting for multiple reasons, not the least of which is its value in re-evaluating the enduring myth that the Utah War was an all-male conflict. We believe the war involved women and girls as well as the males who were their husbands, lovers, relatives, protectors, and occasional tormenters. The war-time story of women on the "home front" and with the troops—Latter-day Saints as well as federals—is largely missing from the history books, just as these accounts have neglected many of the war's colorful characters

---

8   See Truman Capote, *In Cold Blood: A True Account of a Multiple Murder and Its Consequences* (New York: Random House, 1966).

who happened to be men. It is time to surface the adventures of these participants of both genders and opposing sides.

Our hope is that by understanding the Utah War role of Henrietta Polydore and her chronicler, Albert Browne, students of this conflict will also appreciate its sprawling geographical scope. Indeed, it was a territorial-federal confrontation with implications that ranged far beyond Utah and Washington, D.C. to sweep in much of the American West as well as several international locations. That Polydore was the beloved cousin of two of Victorian England's most talented artists of the Pre-Raphaelite Brotherhood—the poet Christina Georgina Rossetti and her painter-brother, Dante Gabriel Rossetti—only enriches her story and those who read it.

Among the descendants of John and Priscilla Alden was a granddaughter, Hannah Bass, who in 1688 married one Joseph Adams, of Braintree, whose descendants at the close of another century became by marriage and inheritance the owners of Mt. Wollaston. There one of them now resides close to where Morton's May-pole stood. It thus happens that while Miles Standish, with ignominious violence, expelled from his home the first master of Merrymount, the last master of Merrymount traces a descent from Miles Standish's successful rival.

Charles Francis Adams, Jr.

THE WARD OF THE THREE GUARDIANS.

I.

On the afternoon of New Year's Day in 1858, the medley of troops, teamsters, and adventurers who composed what was called the Utah Expedition lay huddled in a dreary camp, seven thousand feet above the level of the sea, in the shallow valley of Black's Fork, a few miles south of a little stone redoubt named Fort Bridger, which is still visible from the track of the Pacific railroad. They had marched from the frontier of Missouri in June, confident of entering the Salt Lake Valley before the first bleak storms of the autumn. But the Mormons rose in arms, fortified the canyons which were the avenues to their capital, harassed the army by burning wagon trains and stampeding the quartermaster's cattle, and finally arrested its march in this desolate spot, a hundred and fifty miles east of the Salt Lake, from which it was separated by the massive and snow-bound barrier of the Wasatch Mountains. Between bluffs three or four hundred feet high the river murmured down to the fort under a sheet of ice, and ran zigzag along a strip of bottom-land half a mile wide, which was clad in unbroken snow save in the bends of the stream, where it was dotted with log-huts and tents, from whose chimneys a hundred thin ribbons of smoke floated quietly up into the sky. Among them rose a tall flag-staff, shaped from a mountain pine, on which a starred-and-striped ensign was flapping in the frosty air. A few shivering willow bushes and cottonwoods, despoiled of foliage and charred by fires set by the Mormons, lined the edges of the fork, but no evergreens softened the glare of the landscape, and, besides the streamers of smoke, not a sign of life was visible, except on the flat tops of the bluffs where sentinels were pacing.

Inside of a wide-spreading hospital-tent, which was pitched near the centre of the camp and loomed conspicuously above its neighbors, there was a gathering, this dreary afternoon, whose gayety was in merry contrast with the savage and sombre scenery without. The officers had conspired with the only lady who was sharing the discomforts of the campaign — the wife of the lieutenant-colonel of one of the infantry regiments — to celebrate the day with the best approach Camp Scott could make to the New Year's usages of the Fifth Avenue. The lieutenant-colonel's wife was an older campaigner than most of the conspirators. In fever-hospitals at Vera Cruz, in tangled ambushes among the Everglades, and in all the perils of frontier service, she had followed her husband for twenty years, with a fortitude that rendered her ingenious in the expedients of military life. So in a hospitable chimney built of timber and clay at one end of the tent a huge fire was devouring half a cord of logs; the floor of the pavilion was laid with planks from dismantled wagons; and on a long table built of the same material, and covered with strips of gaudy calico provided by

Atlantic Monthly issue for June 1877
containing Browne's novella
The "Atlantic" was then the leading journal of
literature, art, and politics in the English-speaking world.

Editorial Decisions

*T*HE WARD OF THE THREE GUARDIANS TAKES A helping of fact, adds a dash of fiction, and seasons it throughout with a healthy mixture of both. It is an interesting literary work that has been ignored in the almost century and a half since it was published. Our goal is to help readers tease out the various threads so you can enjoy the entire novella and better understand how Albert Browne created it. The story of *The Ward of the Three Guardians* opens during a New Year's Day party in 1858, a setting that illustrates Browne's talent for mixing truth and fiction to create something akin to fictionalized truth.

TRUTH. General Albert Sidney Johnston, who would earn fame a little over four years later when killed during the Civil War's battle of Shiloh, was indeed present at Camp Scott, Utah Territory on New Year's Day. And it was traditional in that era for social gatherings to occur—in military settings and throughout the nation—on the first day of a new year. In the army, officers customarily extended New Year's greetings during an afternoon "call" at their commanding officer's quarters which makes the story's setting seem accurate, historical, as well as appropriate.[1]

---

1   The tradition of a New Year's Day Call is still followed in many American military organizations today. Large organizations tend to hold such events at the officer's club or open mess instead of the commanding officer's home. See Keith E. Bonn, *Army Officer's Guide*, 50th ed. (Mechanicsburg, Pa.: Stackpole Books, 2005), 16–17.

FICTION. But while the New Year's 1858 party provides a perfect setting for Browne to introduce his story, there is no historical evidence that the reported party actually occurred. General Johnston described provisions as quite sparse in the camp, and he was well known for sharing the hardships of his soldiers.[2] It served Browne's purpose to begin his story with the 1858 New Year's Party, but he apparently had to fictionalize events to do so.

FICTIONALIZED TRUTH. It appears likely, though, that a social gathering of some kind did occur at Camp Scott one week earlier on a very cold Christmas Day in 1857. During that gathering, "One of the officers' ladies had egg nog and a set-out which would have graced any point on the [Atlantic] seaboard."[3] (Since Browne was in camp and almost certainly knew about the Christmas gathering, the question arises as to why he simply did not begin his story one week earlier. The answer is that Johnston did not know he was going to send Browne on a crucial journey east until after Christmas when the captives returned from Salt Lake City with intelligence about Brigham Young's campaign plans.)

While preparing this book, we faced a variety of questions on a wide range of topics as we considered how best to present Browne's novella. A few of those editorial decisions deserve

---

2   Speaking of Albert Sidney Johnston, Maj. Fitz John Porter, who served as Johnston's adjutant during the Utah Expedition's march to Utah, wrote a letter on November 29, 1857, to Irvin McDowell, who would soon command the Department of the Pacific during the Civil War, stating, "We have all endured alike, and the fact that Colonel Johnston has on the march 'footed it,' as did the men; suffers the same exposure, and will not permit the officer to receive more than the soldier, has endeared him to all." Porter to McDowell, "Interesting Information from the Utah Expedition," November 29, 1857, *Washington [D.C.] Union*, January 24, 1858, 2/5–6, in William P. MacKinnon, ed., *At Sword's Point, Part 1: A Documentary History of the Utah War to 1858* (Norman, Okla.: The Arthur H. Clark Company, 2008), 398.

3   Entry for December 25, 1857, Phelps diary transcription, Hamilton Gardner Collection in MacKinnon, ed., *At Sword's Point, Part 1*, 494.

special mention. For example, one judgment we made runs to how best to describe The Church of Jesus Christ of Latter-day Saints and its members. "Mormon" is a longstanding nickname derived from the title of one of the religion's principal scriptures, The Book of Mormon. During much of the nineteenth century the church's leaders often wrote this term in quotes to signify their discomfort with this informality, a reaction quite different than The Society of Friends' acceptance, if not embrace, of the descriptor "Quaker." Several years ago, in order to strengthen its identity as a Christian organization, the church's leadership made clear the use of "Mormon" was to be discouraged and that the organization's formal name was the preferred form of address. The more recent and somewhat slangy term "LDS" was also deemed inappropriate. Accordingly, outside of the novella's six sections, we have attempted to use Latter-day Saint in place of Mormon or LDS whenever appropriate. Conversely, because of its sometimes pejorative flavor, we have also chosen to avoid using "Gentile," the old term in Utah for non-members (even Jewish ones). The editors—one a Latter-day Saint and the other Presbyterian—jointly view these decisions as a matter of respect for our readers and their religious affiliations, if any, rather than an observance of the forces of "political correctness."

The strength of every story depends upon the richness of the plot and the associated characters. In *The Ward of the Three Guardians*, character names are often front and center. Here are five name-related details we want to bring to your attention:

1   HENRIETTA. There are three "Henriettas" woven into this tale—Henrietta Cheek Mayer (the grandmother), Henrietta Mayer Polydore (the mother), and young Henrietta Polydore (the child—who is the actual "ward" in *The Ward of the Three Guardians*).

2   POLYDORE. The family's Italian surname was "Polidori," which is how young Henrietta's paternal grandfather spelled it. Her father, Henry, anglicized it in order, as one of the Rossetti cousins wrote, to attract more legal business. We use "Polydore" because that was the name of young Henrietta and her parents, and was the spelling used in all her case's legal and diplomatic papers.[4]

3   FICTIONALIZED NAMES. Throughout most of the nineteenth century, it was considered poor form to use a person's surname in a literary setting without permission. Accordingly, many novels contain numerous references to "Miss ___" or "Mr. X."[5] Browne chose to conceal slightly the identity of several key figures in his drama by changing their surnames. Thus, Samuel W. Richards became Sam Peckham, Richards' wife Jane Mayer became Jane Moore, and Henrietta Mayer Polydore became Henrietta Perego. Even in his private scrapbook of press clippings, Browne could not bring himself to use David A. Burr's name in the brief note he scrawled for posterity to identify who wrote dispatches for the New-York Tribune while he spent five months traveling to the East and back on a special courier mission. Instead of writing "Burr," he used dashes for the surname. It was apparently permissible, though, to identify fully private people in newspaper reporting. In Browne's 1858 dispatches for the New-York Tribune, he named several such people (Samuel W. Richards, Henry and Henrietta Polydore, and Jane Mayer) who he would

---

4   One such example is "Later from Utah," New-York Daily Tribune, September 6, 1858, 6.
5   See, for example, W. H. Barse to Hon. W. H. Seward, November 26, 1861, in Kenneth L. Alford, ed., Utah and the American Civil War: The Written Record (Norman, Okla.: The Arthur H. Clark Company, 2017), 128–29.

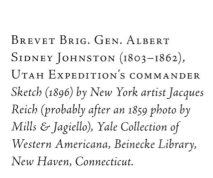

BREVET BRIG. GEN. ALBERT
SIDNEY JOHNSTON (1803–1862),
UTAH EXPEDITION'S COMMANDER
*Sketch (1896) by New York artist Jacques
Reich (probably after an 1859 photo by
Mills & Jagiello), Yale Collection of
Western Americana, Beinecke Library,
New Haven, Connecticut.*

not fully identify in *Ward*, but for whom he instead used disguised names. (See table on page 77.)

4   HISTORICAL FIGURES. Browne mentioned several public or historical figures (Brigham Young, Albert Sidney Johnston, the British foreign minister, Buchanan's cabinet officers, and even Jim Bridger) in his novella and in so doing used their real names as was permissible.

5   RIVERS. We have followed the practice of the U.S. Geological Survey and State of Wyoming in spelling the Green River's tributaries without an apostrophe, as in Blacks and Smiths Fork.

Writing in 1877, Browne identified Albert Sidney Johnston as a "general" throughout his novella, which would have seemed natural to his readers. Johnston was a Confederate general when he was killed at the battle of Shiloh on April 6, 1862. As the senior officer—North or South—killed during the Civil War, Johnston would have been well-known to most of Browne's readers. The fact, though, is that in the U.S. Army Johnston was a colonel until he signed his new oath of office at Camp Scott in April 1858, at which point he became a brevet brigadier, with promotion retroactive to the previous November. To avoid confusion, we—like Browne—have chosen to refer to Johnston as "general" throughout this book.

While *The Ward of the Three Guardians* is heavily truthful, it is important to recognize that numerous inaccuracies also appear in the text. Browne had a special, unique, and valuable view of events, but his perspective was also limited, highly opinionated, and biased. (For example, he favored an army-imposed declaration of martial law in Utah Territory and advocated the lynching of the most senior Latter-day Saint leaders.) Serving as a clerk for Judge Eckels afforded him special access to numerous official documents which may have also informed his views. During the writing of his novella, Browne worked mainly from the dispatches he wrote for the *Tribune* during the Utah War, but his knowledge had its limits. Because Browne lost touch with Henrietta after she returned to England, he had to fabricate an ending for the novella. The literary solution was a return of both parties to Salt Lake City set in 1870, an event that never happened. In creating portions of his narrative out of whole cloth, Browne simply got it "wrong."

Thousands of pages have been written about the Utah War. The challenge faced by the editors of this book is the need for brevity while, at the same time, providing essential background and contextual information surrounding the people, complex events, and circumstances that Browne brought together to form his story. Throughout the novella, the editors will alert readers to such material by providing italicized paragraphs at the beginning of its six sections and additional insights in the accompanying footnotes. Our hope is that doing so will better enable you to enjoy and appreciate Browne's work.

Finally, a word about editorial background and perspective. This presentation of Albert G. Browne's novella is the work of historians who are longtime professional colleagues as well as personal friends. Through shared responsibilities and a mutually forged vision, we have tried mightily to make our effort seamless to avoid the bifurcation marring other collaborations. Although there are substantial differences in our backgrounds, we believe they have enriched and strengthened this study rather than handicapped it. These differences are wide-ranging: matters of generation, regional orientation, education, religious affiliation, ethnicity, military service, and professional experience. What has enabled us to leverage this diversity is a bond of mutual respect linked to a shared commitment to the history of the American West and the significant but sometimes controversial role of Utah's Latter-day Saints. By surfacing *The Ward of the Three Guardians* as we have, we hope to shed light and present truths rather than settle scores or win arguments. In the process, our goal has been to present in edited form one of the Utah War's lamentably neglected primary sources—A. G. Browne, Jr.'s dramatic story of young Henrietta Polydore's adventures among the Latter-day Saints and their adversaries. It is a tale that has been hiding in plain sight since *The Atlantic Monthly* originally published it in 1877, but hidden it has been and for far too long.

WILLIAM P. MACKINNON AND KENNETH L. ALFORD
Montecito, California, and Springville, Utah

Fort Bridger

The Utah Expedition's improvised supply depot and winter quarters
(November 1857–June 1858) 113 miles from Salt Lake City. *Photo (Spring 1858)
by Mills & Jagiello, courtesy Lee-Palfrey Collection, Library of Congress.*

Background and Context

THE UTAH WAR, ALBERT G. BROWNE,
AND HENRIETTA POLYDORE

WHEN HE TOOK UP THE PEN TO WRITE *The Ward of the Three Guardians*, Browne set its opening on New Year's Day 1858 at Camp Scott, the Utah Expedition's winter quarters near the ruins of Fort Bridger in northeastern Utah (now Wyoming). With the army beleaguered by Utah raiders and its troops sheltered in tents at 7,000 feet above sea level, Camp Scott was the largest garrison in North America. What were the political forces that brought about this unprecedented military confrontation in the wilderness? It is an important question, for, without the Utah War, the destinies of *Ward's* author and main protagonist would never have converged. Absent this catalyst, Browne would have continued in Boston as a struggling lawyer with unclear future, and Polydore would have remained in Salt Lake City as a sequestered adolescent-in-exile with prospects for an early marriage—perhaps a polygamous one—among Latter-day Saints.

⚜ The Utah War

In brief, the conflict was the armed confrontation over power and authority between the civil-religious hierarchy of Utah Territory led by Governor Brigham Young, president of the Church of Jesus Christ of Latter-day Saints, and the administration of President James Buchanan.[1] In the spring of 1857, soon after his inauguration, Buchanan perceived rebellion and set out to restore federal authority in the territory by replacing Young as governor and installing a successor to be escorted west by a large army expeditionary force. It was a change Young contested through his Nauvoo Legion and the use of hit-and-run guerrilla tactics. The result was a bloody conflict that brought not only casualties but federal treason indictments for Young and hundreds of other Latter-day Saints. For the former governor and a few others, there would also be indictments for murder. With tens of thousands of troops and camp followers involved, it was the nation's most extensive and expensive military undertaking during the period between the Mexican-American and Civil Wars.

At the heart of the conflict was the disconnect between the two leaders' radically different philosophies of governance. Young viewed Utah as a millennially focused theocracy operating under his prophetic, authoritarian leadership. The U.S. government saw Utah as one among multiple federal territories intended to function under republican principles and, until statehood, as a ward of Congress through a federally sworn governor appointed

---

1   For the most recent scholarship on the war, from which this summary is derived, see MacKinnon, ed., *At Sword's Point, Part 1* and *Part 2*; David L. Bigler and Will Bagley, *The Mormon Rebellion: America's First Civil War, 1857–1858* (Norman: University of Oklahoma Press, 2011); Ronald W. Walker, Richard E. Turley Jr., and Glen M. Leonard, *Massacre at Mountain Meadows* (New York: Oxford University Press, 2008); and Norman F. Furniss, *The Mormon Conflict, 1850–1859* (New Haven, Conn.: Yale University Press, 1960).

by the president, confirmed by the senate, and supervised by the U.S. secretary of state.

The war did not well up abruptly in the spring of 1857 because of a single critical incident. Instead, it arose from ten years of accumulated issues, with Utah-federal relations steadily deteriorating after the Latter-day Saints' 1847 arrival in the Salt Lake Valley, then a part of Mexican Alta California, after enduring persecution in Illinois, Missouri, and elsewhere. A failed attempt by President Franklin Pierce to replace Young as governor during 1854–55 was emblematic of both the growing tensions involved and the fecklessness of Buchanan's predecessors in dealing with them. By Buchanan's inauguration on March 4, 1857, virtually every area of contact between Utahns and the U.S. government had become a contest of wills. Conflicts that arose over administration of departmental matters such as mail service were aggravated by public uproar over three emotional issues: the church's official acknowledgement of polygamy in 1852 after years of denial; the new Republican Party's adoption of an anti-polygamy presidential platform plank in 1856; and perceptions that Brigham Young was seeking independence outside the Union while arranging anti-federal alliances with multiple Indian tribes. The latter was especially volatile because of its potential for bloodshed and blockage of the transcontinental emigration trails to the Pacific Coast as well as the fact that Young had long doubled as Utah's U.S. superintendent of Indian affairs.

Catalyst for President Buchanan's decision-making at the end of March 1857 was a series of complaints by Utah's federal appointees, virtually all of whom (except Brigham Young) would flee the territory in early April. Theirs was the second such exodus in five years. These officials portrayed Utah as a violent territory led by a disloyal, out-of-control governor prone to incendiary rhetoric

PRESIDENT JAMES BUCHANAN AND CABINET, CA. 1859
Photo montage by Mathew Brady, courtesy National Archives.

disrespectful of the U.S. government. In the Latter-day Saint view, such provocative language from their civil and religious leader was simply an assertion of Utah's constitutional rights in the face of congressional and executive branch behavior perceived in the Great Basin as colonial, corrupt, and ineffective.

Because of enduring controversies enveloping the Utah War's historiography, understanding what the conflict *was not* is important to grasping what it *was*. Despite Latter-day Saint complaints of religious persecution, the Utah War was not a federal attack on the Church of Jesus Christ of Latter-day Saints or its religious tenets. As unpopular as the polygamy issue was across the country, in 1857 there was no U.S. statute barring the practice of plural marriage. For a lawyerly James Buchanan, the issue in Utah was a restoration of federal authority, not eradication of polygamy or its practitioners. His orders to Gen. Albert Sidney Johnston, commander of the Utah Expedition, and the new governor, Alfred Cumming of Georgia, reflected this emphasis.

If the Utah War was not a religious crusade, neither was it an affair described by the church until quite recently as "bloodless." Such a trivialization obscured the enormity of the September 11, 1857, Mountain Meadows massacre; it was an atrocity in which Nauvoo Legionnaires and their Southern Paiute auxiliaries disarmed and killed about 120 Arkansans emigrating to California through southern Utah, one of the great blood-lettings of the entire American overland trails experience. This atrocity plus a plethora of smaller-scale killings produced casualties roughly equivalent to those in the territory's eastern neighbor, dubbed "Bleeding Kansas."

Four days after the tragedy at Mountain Meadows, Brigham Young proclaimed martial law, an illegal decree that barred civilians and the U.S. Army from entering, crossing, or even leaving Utah Territory without his authorization. News of this draconian move and shock over the massacre halted migration to California and Oregon, an intolerable problem for a westering nation accustomed to the freedom of unrestricted travel.

In mid-October Brigham Young issued secret orders to the Nauvoo Legion authorizing the use of lethal force against the Utah Expedition if it moved west of Fort Bridger toward the Salt Lake Valley. With this escalation, the appalling loss of life at Mountain Meadows, the destructive, million-dollar raids on the U.S. Army's livestock and supply trains, and the imposition of martial law, Brigham Young crossed a Rubicon in the fall of 1857. In so doing, he changed the character of his dispute with the U.S. government from a series of nasty provocations to armed rebellion.

During the third week of November, the Utah Expedition reached Blacks Fork of the Green River after crossing the Continental Divide at South Pass and enduring Latter-day Saint attacks, agonizing cold, blizzards, and a massive loss of beef cattle and draught animals. There, near the ruins of Fort Bridger, a civilian trading post burned by the Nauvoo Legion in October, Albert Sidney Johnston concluded that he could not force the snow-clogged mountain passes into the Salt Lake Valley only 113 miles to the southwest. At an altitude of 7,000 feet above sea level, he took his exhausted command into winter quarters, designating the vast cantonment he established as Camp Scott in honor of the army's general in chief.

On December 8 President Buchanan sent his first annual message to Congress. In that document—now known as the State of the Union Address—he commented that in Utah the United States faced its first territorial rebellion and that he intended to suppress it "in such a manner that it shall be the last."[2] By month-

---

2   James Buchanan, "First Annual Message to Congress," December 8, 1857, Moore, ed., *The Works of James Buchanan*, 10:129–63, and in reference to Utah in MacKinnon, *At Sword's Point, Part 1*, 481–84.

end, Camp Scott was electrified by news brought with the return of several Utah Expedition soldiers and civilian teamsters held captive for months in Salt Lake City. Upon debriefing these former prisoners of war, General Johnston learned that Brigham Young was forming a new 1,000-man cavalry brigade of regulars—the Standing Army of Israel—to reinforce the Nauvoo Legion's militia troops. According to this intelligence windfall, Young intended to use the Standing Army to intercept the army's reinforcements en route from New Mexico Territory as well as to spearhead a surprise assault on first Camp Scott and then Fort Laramie, Nebraska Territory, planned for the spring of 1858. As the year turned over, the question preoccupying the Utah Expedition's winter quarters was how Johnston would react to this new threat.

🟖 ALBERT G. BROWNE, JR.

When *Ward* appeared in June 1877, Browne was hardly an unknown. Not only was he a prominent Manhattan newspaper editor, tormentor of New York's corrupt mayor, William Marcy ("Boss") Tweed, and former military secretary to Massachusetts' Civil War governor, he had standing as author of the most authoritative account of the Utah War to date: *The Atlantic Monthly's* three-part series of 1859 titled "The Utah Expedition: Its Causes and Consequences."[3] So comprehensive was this study, historians then and now have viewed it as among the most important primary sources of information about the war. What has not been well understood is that during 1857–58 Browne had accompanied

---

3   Anonymous [Albert G. Browne, Jr.], "The Utah Expedition: Its Causes and Consequences," *The Atlantic Monthly. A Magazine of Literature, Art, and Politics* 3 (March–May 1859): 361–75, 474–91, 570–84. Browne was formally identified as the author of this three-part article only with the appearance of *The Atlantic Monthly's* first cumulative index in the 1880s, although his responsibility for the piece was an open secret, at least in Boston, soon after its publication.

ALBERT GALLATIN BROWNE, JR. (1835–1891)

Images depict Browne at various stages of his life: as a boy in Salem, Massachusetts (1841), a graduating senior at Cambridge's Harvard College (1853), a Boston attorney (1859–1861), a Union Army lieutenant colonel and military secretary to the Bay State's governor (1863), and a newspaperman in New York (1884) shortly before returning to Boston in 1887 and becoming a banker before falling victim to the diabetes his wife and Harvard classmates believed stemmed from the hardships of his experiences in Utah. *Images courtesy of multiple Harvard libraries as well as Browne family descendants Katherine Greenough, Robert Chamberlin, and Charles Browne residing in such disparate places as Boston, Houston, and Richmond, Virginia.*

the Utah Expedition to write long, unsigned dispatches about virtually every aspect of the war for Horace Greeley's *New-York Tribune*. It was this experience as a correspondent at the hub of things that enabled Browne to write "Causes and Consequences" in 1859 and then *Ward* nearly twenty years later.

Who was Albert G. Browne, Jr. and how at age twenty-two did he become a war correspondent for one of the nation's leading newspapers? Browne has no biographer, and this study is not the place to remedy that shortfall except selectively.[4] Suffice it to say that when the Utah War arose in the spring of 1857, he was a young, well-educated, unmarried native of Salem, Massachusetts, in search of his future and open to suggestion. Scion of one of Salem's patrician but not wealthy families, he and his father were the namesake of President Thomas Jefferson's Swiss-born secretary of the treasury, Albert Gallatin. Albert's father was a successful ship chandler, a businessman furnishing provisions, hardware, and rope to Salem's venerable maritime industry while mingling on familiar terms with the Brahmins of nearby Boston. His was a business with a patina of romance, serving as it did the clipper ships of the centuries-old China tea trade as well as the less elegant vessels rounding Cape Horn to exploit first California's hide-and-tallow commerce and then the needs of the gold rush. Young Albert had little interest in such work; by the

---

4　The latest biographical sketch of Browne is MacKinnon, "Vita: Albert Gallatin Browne, Jr., A Brief Life of an Early War Correspondent: 1832 [1835]–1891," *Harvard Magazine* 111 (November–December 2008): 48–49. Much of the balance of this section was developed from two sources: a memorial essay written in the early twentieth century by Browne's Harvard classmates from material provided by his widow; and his family's voluminous papers. See "Albert Gallatin Browne," *Report of the Harvard Class of 1853, 1849–1913, Issued on the Sixtieth Anniversary for the Use of the Class and Its Friends* (Cambridge, Mass.: [Harvard] University Press, 1913), 46–51; and Browne Family Papers, 1802–1962, MC 298, Schlesinger Library, Radcliffe Institute, Harvard University, Cambridge.

mid-1850s, two other forces were shaping his character, talents, and interests: the impact of his education; and involvement in New England's movement to abolish slavery.

Albert's early education was in Salem's private schools. In 1848, at age thirteen, he was prepared to enter Harvard College, but was persuaded to wait a year by his father to continue with tutors in Salem. Upon matriculating in 1849, he was still the youngest member of his class. Although a precocious lad, Browne's passage through Harvard was less than smooth. Early on, a combination of inattention to his studies and undisciplined behavior resulted in his "rustication" or suspension from Harvard for a year. Having successfully refocused his intellect and curbed his impulsiveness in Salem under the supervision of a tutor, a more mature Albert returned to Harvard in 1851 and graduated with his class in 1853. With BA degree in hand, he then embarked on the study of law at Cambridge's Dana Hall, a precursor to Harvard Law School. He also "read law" in the Boston office of John A. Andrew, a rising attorney and political figure who became his mentor.[5]

In the midst of his legal studies, Albert's interest in abolitionism intensified, stimulated in part by the example of his father's role in that movement with such nationally prominent opponents of slavery as U.S. senator Charles Sumner of Massachusetts and New York publisher-editor Horace Greeley. In May 1854 Browne, Jr. was among the leaders of a Boston mob seeking to free escaped Virginia slave Anthony Burns from federal officers enforcing the onerous Fugitive Slave Act. When a city constable died in the melee to free Burns, Albert and several of Boston's most

---

5   Browne's Harvard academic record and a long list of his disciplinary infractions during 1849–50 are included in Albert G. Browne, Jr. records (HUG 300) and Index to University Records, Harvard University Archives, Pusey Library, Cambridge.

prominent abolitionists were indicted for homicide.[6] Although the charges were dropped, Browne and his family felt it advisable for him to leave Boston, go to Europe, and pursue a Ph.D. degree at the University of Heidelberg.

While it is tempting to assume that Browne's European sojourn was prompted by his very recent involvement in the Burns imbroglio, his brother provided a different explanation a half-century later:

> This in no way was the cause of his leaving the Law School. His inclination had always been toward journalism, and when at Heidelberg he took a degree of Ph.D. instead of one in law. His classmate and chum at Harvard, Mr. Charles Blake, and also his classmate Wilder Dwight, were at Heidelberg, and I think this may have had some influence in his forming the desire to take the Heidelberg course. He had the feeling that graduating at so early an age from college was a mistake, and he desired further study before entering upon a profession.[7]

<hr>

6   For the Anthony Burns affair and Browne's role in it, see Albert J. von Frank, *The Trials of Anthony Burns, Freedom and Slavery in Emerson's Boston* (Cambridge, Mass.: Harvard University Press, 1998).

7   Charles Frederick Blake was Browne's friend from childhood and a classmate at both Salem Latin School and Harvard College. As Harvard undergraduates, Blake and Browne were both elected to the exclusive Rumford Society. After the two men received their doctorates at Heidelberg (Blake a JD degree and Browne a Ph.D.), they returned to Boston to practice law and then years later gravitated to New York. Wilder Dwight of Springfield began the study of law immediately after his graduation from Harvard College in 1853, and, like Blake and Browne, interrupted his studies to travel in Europe. Like them, he later returned to Boston, completed his legal studies and apprenticeship (but not in John A. Andrew's office), and practiced there until the Civil War in which he died at Antietam. Edward C. Browne to Samuel S. Shaw, April 27, 1903, Albert G. Browne, Jr. File, Records of the [Harvard] Class of 1853 Secretary, HUD 253.505, Box 62, Harvard University Archives, Pusey Library, Cambridge. As context, see John T. Krumpelmann, "The American Students of Heidelberg University, 1830–1870," *Jahrbuch fur Amerikastudien* 14 (1969): 167–84.

In Germany Albert struggled not only with a rigorous academic program conducted in a new language but with the challenge of defining a career. Notwithstanding his earlier legal studies, he was ambivalent about the prospect of life as an attorney, and so at Heidelberg he chose to study the liberal arts rather than pursue a JD degree. He also began to explore the possibility of a career in journalism and was interested enough in that field to write several unsolicited travel dispatches for European journals while toying with the possibility of generating such material for American newspapers. By January 1855, without such ties in the United States, Browne had given up the notion of journalism as an impractical distraction. All of this Browne, Sr. reported to Senator Sumner, his son's mentor, with evident parental relief: "He has abandoned the idea of writing for any American newspaper. He says he has neither the time nor inclination. I am glad of it, as I do not wish his attention diverted from his studies, however desirable the compensation he might receive would be."[8]

By January 1856 Albert was back in Boston as a newly minted Ph.D. (summa cum laude), telling Senator Sumner, "I had looked forward during last year to passing a portion of the present winter in Washington. I should see it now perhaps with clearer eyes than those of a boy four years ago. But I cannot. I must learn to love the law from necessity, for I cannot from choice." Later that year he completed his legal apprenticeship with attorney Andrew, was admitted to the Massachusetts bar, and received an AM degree from Harvard.[9]

A year later Albert was still uncertain about his life's work.

---

8   Albert G. Browne, Sr. to Charles Sumner, January 3, 1855, Beverly Wilson Palmer, ed., *The Papers of Charles Sumner* (Alexandria, Va.: Chadwyck-Healy, 1988), microfilm reel 12, frame 034.

9   Albert G. Browne, Jr. to Charles Sumner, January 22, 1856, ibid, frame 680.

While sightseeing in Kentucky during June 1857 he visited the editor of Louisville's *Evening Bulletin*, representing himself as affiliated in some undefined way with a Boston newspaper, the *Traveller*. Albert's brother, Edward, later claimed that "on his return from Europe he finished his law studies with John A. Andrew and was connected with Robert Carter in editing the *Boston Atlas*."[10]

And then suddenly the *New-York Tribune* appointed Browne its field correspondent attached to the army's newly organized Utah Expedition. His salary was to be $200 per month, substantial compensation that approximated the pay of a territorial governor like Brigham Young.[11] In many respects, the decision to hire Browne for this assignment was counter-intuitive. He was certainly a literate person, but he had no sustained employment history with newspapers, was without military experience, had never been west of the Mississippi, and may have lacked even basic proficiency in horsemanship. Although his hometown of Salem had linkages to some of Mormonism's second- and third-tier leaders, there is no indication that these community connections would have enabled Browne, a conventional Protestant, to

10 For a summary of Browne's academic record in Germany (much of it recorded in Latin), see Dr. Hans Ewald Kessler of Heidelberg University, email to MacKinnon, March 27, 2002, copy in MacKinnon's research files. Heidelberg did not require Browne to research and write a doctoral dissertation, hence the relatively short period of his degree program. Browne's trip to Kentucky, taken in company with young Charles Hale of the Boston *Advertiser* and largely duplicating one taken two years earlier by Albert's mentor, Senator Sumner, was reported in Louisville *Evening Bulletin*, June 6, 1857, p. 1/col. 2. For the Browne-Carter relationship, see Edward C. Browne to Samuel S. Shaw, April 27, 1903, Albert G. Browne, Jr. File, Records of the [Harvard] Class of 1853 Secretary.

11 Browne's appointment and compensation were so unusual, Brigham Young's principal source of intelligence from Washington (Utah's territorial delegate in Congress) reported it to him. John M. Bernhisel to Brigham Young, November 2, 1857, Church History Library.

present himself as an authority on the Latter-day Saints. The key to understanding the origins of Browne's connection to the *Tribune* lies with an appreciation of the power of serendipity and linkages. Just as the newspaper's New York editors were about to offer their Utah assignment to John Townsend Trowbridge, an experienced Boston journalist and editor with seven published novels to his credit, the *Tribune*'s correspondent in Washington, Robert Carter, intervened gratuitously to deflect the offer to Trowbridge while successfully making the case for engaging Browne, his personal friend and protege.[12]

When Browne joined the *Tribune*, its editorial staff consisted of a managing editor, ten associate editors, and about forty reporters and correspondents. One historian of the New York newspaper scene concluded, "The *Tribune* became famous because Horace Greeley attracted and trained an exceptionally talented staff. One *Tribune* writer, John Russell Young, called his coworkers 'resolute, brilliant, capable, irresponsible, intolerant—not above setting things on fire for the fun of seeing them burn.' E. L. Godkin recalled that 'admission to the columns of the *Tribune*

---

12   Trowbridge later came to view the selection of Browne rather than him as a blessing: "I forgave this act of Carter's at the time, and ever afterwards had reason to be rather glad of it, on learning what hardships befell the expedition, when, in the following winter, it so narrowly missed the fate of Napoleon's army in its retreat from Russia. Browne accompanied it in my place, and wrote an excellent account of it [in 1859] . . . a history I used to fancy I might have written myself but for Carter's interposition. Browne had a more robust constitution than mine, a fact that may have influenced the elder man in choosing between us; and, looking back now upon the event, I am inclined to think that, if I had gone with the expedition, I should not have been in the way of writing that history, or ever anything else, after the terrible Utah business." In view of Trowbridge's long editorial career at *The Atlantic Monthly*, it would be interesting to know if he played any role in selecting *Ward* for publication twenty years later. John Townsend Trowbridge, "An Early Contributor's Recollections," *The Atlantic Monthly* 100 (July 1907): 582.

almost gave the young writer a patent of literary nobility.' Greeley staffed his paper with intellectuals."[13]

By late August 1857 Browne was westbound on the Oregon-California Trail in Nebraska, lugging a carpet bag across the plains under the protection of the army's Utah Expedition. His dispatches from the trail and earlier from Fort Leavenworth, Kansas, described what he saw around him: prominent rock formations, the weather, lynchings, Indian encampments and raids, buffalo stampedes, and military posts. He also reported rumors drifting east about Utah's war preparations. At Fort Kearny he took time from his *Tribune* responsibilities to urge Senator Sumner to promote recently wounded 1st Lt. J. E. B. Stuart of the First U.S. Cavalry, a regiment in the field commanded by Sumner's cousin. It was a recommendation that with hindsight seems unthinkable, with Stuart soon serving as one of the Confederacy's senior cavalry leaders and Browne a lieutenant colonel in the Union Army.[14]

If Brigham Young crossed a political Rubicon of sorts in the late summer and fall of 1857, so too did Albert in terms of the intensity of his hostility to Mormonism. The further west he moved, the more emotional he became on the subject, blurring

---

13   Catherine C. Mitchell, ed., *Margaret Fuller's New York Journalism: A Biographical Essay and Key Writings* (Knoxville: University of Tennessee Press, 1995), 10–11.

14   Albert G. Browne, Jr. to Charles Sumner, August 30, 1857, Palmer, ed., *The Papers of Charles Sumner*, microfilm reel 16, frames 029–30. Lieutenant Stuart was not promoted to captain until April 22, 1861 in an unsuccessful attempt to forestall his resignation at the beginning of the Civil War.

    Based on the similarity of names and the Polydore family's presence in Louisiana before, during, and after the Civil War there is a high probability—and an element of irony—that two of Henrietta Polydore's uncles served as privates in the Confederate army. Louisiana's Confederate States Zouave Battalion lists Charles Mayer, who served in Company C, and John Mayer, who served in Company A. See "War Department Collection of Confederate Records (Louisiana)," National Archives and Records Administration, Record Group 109, Microfilm 378, Roll 19 (Washington, D.C.).

DELANA R. ECKELS (1806–1888),
UTAH'S CONTROVERSIAL CHIEF JUSTICE
Viewed negatively by Latter-day Saints for his
hostility to polygamy, he presided at the August
1858 trial that led to Henrietta's repatriation and
then escorted her and Aunt Jane cross-country
to the British legation in Washington. *Pre–Civil
War photo used by permission, Utah State Historical
Society.*

the role of a reporter with that of an editor or polemicist. After learning of Young's actions in October, Browne wrote the *Tribune,* "In the present crisis there is no longer room for child's play. There is but one alternative. Either the laws of the United States are to be subverted and its territory appropriated by a gang of traitorous lechers, who have declared themselves to constitute 'a free and independent state,' or Salt Lake City must be entered at the point of a bayonet, and the ringleaders of the Mormon rebellion seized and hung." It was fervor of the sort that propelled him to the front of the crowd seeking Anthony Burns' freedom three years earlier while fueling current Latter-day Saint anxieties about army intentions and lynch mobs.[15]

When the Utah Expedition was forced into winter quarters at Camp Scott in late November, Albert Browne remained with the army, barred by General Johnston from attempting to reach Salt Lake City on his own. Almost immediately he obtained

---

15   [Browne] "Later From the Mormon War," Dispatch, Camp on Blacks Fork, November 5, 1857, *New-York Tribune*, December 28, 1857.

appointment as clerk to Delana R. Eckels of Indiana, the chief justice of Utah's supreme court who had also travelled west with the army. As with his employment by New York's *Tribune*, Browne's connection to Judge Eckels at Camp Scott was serendipitous, the result of camaraderie forged at Fort Leavenworth and along the Oregon-California Trail. Despite the difference in their age and regional background, a bond between the two men also developed from their common interest in the law and journalism. Eckels was aware that Albert was writing for the *Tribune*; whether Browne realized that the judge was sending dispatches as "Kenton" to Cincinnati's *Enquirer* is unknown.[16] Through his deep involvement with Judge Eckels and his court, Browne had extraordinary access to information, perspective, and documents unavailable to his competitors among Camp Scott's other newspaper reporters.

From this privileged perch in the wilderness, Browne continued to produce a steady flow of letters to the *Tribune*. It is no surprise that when a federal grand jury sitting at Fort Bridger during December indicted Brigham Young and other Latter-day Saint leaders for treason, Browne scooped other reporters by obtaining a copy of the indictment. Such was also the case with the intelligence obtained from the prisoners returned to the army from Latter-day Saint captivity at year-end. So informative and colorful were his dispatches, the *Tribune* published them on its front page but did so without attribution, identifying Albert's work opaquely as "our special correspondence." When issues of the *Tribune* carrying this material washed back into Camp Scott

16   Judge Eckels' newspaper dispatches as "Kenton" are unknown to historians of the Utah War and therefore remain unanalyzed. The only description of them is a brief one in MacKinnon, "Epilogue to the Utah War: Impact and Legacy," *Journal of Mormon History* 29 (Fall 2003): 234–35. When the judge tired of this role, another of his proteges, Washington Jay McCormick (like Browne, a lawyer), took up the pen for Cincinnati's *Enquirer* as "Kenton, Jr."

courtesy of westbound travelers and the U.S. mail, they immediately became "must" reading for soldiers of all ranks at one end
of the sprawling encampment hungry for an insider's news of the
doings at the other end.[17] Although Browne wrote anonymously,
Camp Scott's troops and camp followers soon identified him as
the author. So too did Brigham Young, fuming over his press
coverage in Salt Lake City's Lion House.

From these dynamics came a surprise on New Year's Day 1858
that changed Albert Browne's life.

⚜ HENRIETTA POLYDORE

If in 1877 some readers of *The Atlantic Monthly* recognized Browne's
name, Henrietta Polydore's name was not a familiar one. Today
the world remembers her, if at all, as namesake for a thirty-one-
foot sloop berthed at a sailing club on England's Devon coast.[18]

---

17   For a laudatory view of Browne's reporting from Camp Scott, see [Capt. Albert Tracy]
"T" to "N," "A Letter from the Utah Army," December 10, 1857, *Commercial Advertiser*
(Buffalo, N.Y.), February 3, 1858, 2/1–2: "The New York *Tribune* has a correspondent
in camp. It being his business to pick up news, he doubtless gathers many items of
which I may hear nothing in so large a camp as this. . . . From some acquaintance with
its correspondent here, I think he will only state facts, or what he believes to be facts. I
understand the campaign on Ham's Fork was served up and sent forward by last mail,
and that the controlling spirit in that lusterless performance has been handled without gloves. I hope the simple facts have been related: they are quite sufficient, without
varnish. I wish you would send me copies of the *Tribune* containing letters from Utah."
This letter is reprinted in MacKinnon, ed., *At Sword's Point, Part 1*, 456.

18   The *Henrietta Polydore* is owned by Miles and Jill Butler of Devon and is home
ported at the Topsham Sailing Club on the River Dart. When they bought the boat
they retained its name, aware of its namesake's connection to the Rossettis but not
her sojourn in Utah Territory.
     There is no biography of Henrietta. This sketch of her childhood in England
and her sequestration in Utah through 1858 has been assembled by research in the
papers of her Rossetti cousins (William and Dante), and Jill Waller, "Christina
Rossetti's Cheltenham Connection," *Cheltenham Local History Journal* 18 (2002):
70–74. Also essential has been the correspondence of her mother (Henrietta

THE SLOOP
HENRIETTA POLYDORE
This ocean-going pleasure craft,
home ported along England's River
Dart, is one of the few modern
evocations of the beloved cousin
commemorated in the Rossetti
siblings' Pre-Raphaelite poetry and
art during the mid-1800s. *Photo
courtesy of boat owners Miles and Jill
Butler, Devon, England.*

The roots of Henrietta's Utah sojourn go back to at least 1843 when her parents, Henry Francis Polydore and Henrietta Mayer, married as Roman Catholics in London, where he practiced law as a solicitor. Henry's mother was English and his father Italian; his bride belonged to a large provincial family in Cheltenham, a small coastal city in Gloucestershire. By virtue of Henry Polydore's sister's earlier marriage to Gabriele Rossetti, an intellectual but revolutionary refugee from Naples, the newlyweds were immediately connected to London's community of Italian political exiles, of whom Rossetti was the leader.

After a few years of marriage, the Polydores moved to Gloucestershire in hopes of growing Henry's legal practice. In 1846 they had their first and only child, a daughter named Henrietta in honor of both her mother and grandmother Mayer. Despite this relocation, the girl became close to her Rossetti cousins

---

Mayer Polydore) and aunt (Jane Mayer Richards), and the journal and letters of Jane's polygamous husband (Samuel W. Richards), as well as the diplomatic and court records associated with young Henrietta's repatriation in 1858. See especially Samuel Whitney Richards Papers 1837–1929, MS 6576, Box 1, Folder 13; Samuel W. Richards Journal 1857–1858, MS 1841; and Jane Mayer Richards Correspondence 1857–1867, MS 3528, all Church History Library.

HENRY FRANCIS POLYDORE
(1808–1885), YOUNG HENRIETTA'S
DOUR, LAWYERLY FATHER
Sketched in 1855 by nephew Dante
Gabriel Rossetti as Henrietta traveled
secretly to Utah with his estranged wife
and her sister. *Courtesy Alamy Photos.*

in London, especially two who would develop into leaders of England's Pre-Raphaelite Brotherhood, a movement of highly talented intellectuals, artists, and craftsmen: Christina Georgina Rossetti, a brilliant poet, and her brother, Dante Gabriel Rossetti, a prominent painter. In 1849 Christina wrote "To Lalla," a poem inspired by three-year-old Henrietta and titled for her pet name within the family. (See Appendix A.)

As these Anglo-Italian cousins grew close, Henrietta's parents became incompatible. By 1851 only Henry and their daughter were living together in the town of Gloucester; his wife was presumably residing in Cheltenham or elsewhere in the county, perhaps tending one of the Mayer family's multiple businesses. A London cousin, William Michael Rossetti, later described life among the Polydores as "turbulent" and father Henry as "a man of narrow nature, kindly in an ordinary degree, punctiliously conscientious: in this respect I think he exceeded all other men I have known, having more of the scrupulosity of some women. A strict Catholic devout in practice." In William's view, mother Henrietta Mayer Polydore was temperamentally quite different than her husband, being "a somewhat curious character, with lots of business energy and [the] power of [landing] on her feet in risky places. . . . the daughter of a Baker in Cheltenham [with] an ordinary amount of education and culture." Dante Gabriel Rossetti viewed Henry as "an old fogey" and tried to avoid him when Henry visited London.[19]

In 1852 Mrs. Polydore, her parents, and many of her Mayer siblings converted from Catholicism to Mormonism, a change that further strained the Polydore marriage since Henry remained a staunch Catholic. In spite of the church's shocking admission that year to the practice of plural marriage, it was a time of explosive growth for the Latter-day Saints. Fueling this expansion was the strong appeal of the church's millennialism amidst the appalling living and working conditions of Great Britain's industrial revolution and the political instability surrounding the approaching Crimean War.

Coincident with and capitalizing on this ferment was the presence of some of the Latter-day Saints' most effective American missionary-leaders, including Samuel W. Richards, a charismatic man still in his mid-twenties when he became president of the British Mission during 1852. Samuel was a member of Mormonism's Utah "aristocracy," a nephew of Willard Richards, a cousin and second counselor to Brigham Young in the church's First Presidency. His wife remained in Utah. How and when Richards caught the attention of little Henrietta's unmarried and strikingly attractive maternal aunt, Jane Elizabeth Mayer, is unknown, but he surely did. Some sort of romantic attraction developed facilitated by their common religion. Unlike Richards' socializing with other women under the mission's jurisdiction to whom he was attracted, like Helena L. Robinson who later became his third wife, Samuel was extremely circumspect about his interest in Jane Mayer. He did not mention her in his journal until the summer of 1855.

The next act in this complex drama came in March 1854 when

---

19   The Rossettis' characterizations of Henry and Henrietta Mayer Polydore may be found in Antony H. Harrison, ed., *The Letters of Christina Rossetti*, 4 vols. (Charlottesville: The University of Virginia Press, 1997), 1 (1843–73): 52n1.

Mrs. Polydore abruptly withdrew eight-year-old Henrietta from her Catholic boarding school in Lincolnshire and secretly fled via Liverpool to the United States with her daughter and sister Jane. Significantly, it was a time when Samuel W. Richards knew that release from his mission and return to Utah were imminent. Once Henry Polydore became aware of his family's departure from Lincolnshire, he immediately suspected they would head for Liverpool, the major port of embarkation for British Latter-day Saints emigrating to the United States. In a near-frenzy, he enlisted the help of his relatives in London, writing his nephew, Dante Rossetti,

> if [your brother] William can without inconvenience come down hither and remain with me for a short time in order to advise & aid in the strenuous endeavours I am making to find and regain possession of your "cousin" his so doing will be of great service to me & the sooner I see him the better . . . I cannot promise to be here on his arrival as I may at any moment be summoned to Liverpool or else whither . . . Should I be summoned from home I should find William most serviceable in *either* of two ways—1st should he accompany me, to aid me in seeking for and regaining possession of the child & 2nd, should he remain here, in seeing the police or other *callers* & attending to my instructions from the place at which I may be stationed.

Dante, in turn, informed his brother William, "Uncle Henry thinks too he has discovered in Liverpool the residence of some . . . friends of H.'s: (thus) it seems they are on the point of sailing for N. Orleans."[20]

Meanwhile Samuel Richards had been working to organize the departure on April 4 of a 220-person company of Latter-day Saint converts aboard *Germanicus*, a square-rigged sailing vessel out of Thomaston, Maine, on which Jane Mayer and the two

---

20 Henry F. Polydore to Dante Rossetti quoted in Rossetti to William Michael Rossetti, March 27, 1854, ibid, 1:96.

Henriettas booked passage to New Orleans. They used a ticket pre-arranged by someone in the Salt Lake Valley and financed through the church's Perpetual Emigrating Fund. There are hints in Samuel Richards' journal and PEF's records that at some point young Henrietta may have balked at the prospect of crossing the Atlantic. If so, her hesitation was resolved, and she sailed with her mother and aunt on *Germanicus*.[21] Henry Polydore's descent on Liverpool's docks was too late.

The three women in the Polydore-Mayer party arrived in New Orleans on June 12 after a long but largely uneventful voyage that required them to touch port at Grand Caicos Island and Florida's Dry Tortugas to take on fresh water. Once in Louisiana, they ascended the Mississippi by steamer to St. Louis. There, for reasons that are unclear, they and others who had emigrated aboard *Germanicus* remained quasi-marooned for a year until the late summer of 1855. At that time they apparently managed to join a wagon train bound for Salt Lake City, perhaps the one arranged by Samuel and his business partners to transport machinery for a mill they were building. How Jane and her relatives sustained themselves among the local Latter-day Saints during this sojourn in St. Louis is another of the intriguing gaps in the story of their emigration to Utah.

Notwithstanding Samuel Richards' romantic interest in Jane Mayer, he did not cross the Atlantic with her. Duty dictated that

---

21   Details of the Polydore-Mayer party's trans-Atlantic passage and how it was financed are murky. What is known of their ticketing and presumed sailing aboard *Germanicus* comes from British Mission (Liverpool Office). Emigration Records. Emigration Book C, 82–95; Folio in Application Book:56, Ticket No. 238, PEF Bond 685. For information about *Germanicus* and her Liverpool–New Orleans voyage in the spring of 1854, see Fred Woods and Blaine Blake, comps., *The LDS Emigrant Roster and Voyage History, Crossing the Ocean, 1840–1869* (privately published CD). Information transcribed and transmitted via Ardis E. Parshall to MacKinnon, email message of August 3, 2002, copy in MacKinnon's research files.

he remain in England for several more weeks until his brother, Franklin D. Richards, arrived from Salt Lake City to assume leadership of the British Mission. Once properly relieved of this responsibility, Samuel sailed to Boston, traveled by rail to the Missouri River, and, using the overland trail, arrived in Salt Lake City during September 1854. He spent the winter of 1854–55 resuming active operation of his mercantile and agricultural properties and completing renovation of his house, presumably in anticipation of an expansion to his family. In February 1855 he took a second wife, the fifteen-year-old niece of the first wife he had married in Nauvoo in 1846. During the summer Samuel's journal reflects time spent corresponding jointly with Jane and her sister Henrietta, presumably still in St. Louis. Upon reaching Salt Lake City sometime in the fall of 1855, the women of the Polydore-Mayer party took up lodgings, but where, how, and with what understandings is not known. It was, however, a time during which Samuel later described himself as being under considerable financial pressure. Notwithstanding these circumstances, on February 16, 1856, Samuel arranged for Brigham Young to marry him to both Jane E. Mayer and Helena L. Robinson, with Helena designated his third wife and Jane the fourth.[22]

During the spring of 1856, Henrietta Mayer Polydore left her daughter in sister Jane's care, re-crossed the plains, and sailed to England from New Orleans to prepare her aging parents in Cheltenham as well as at least five of her ten siblings for emigration to the United States. That she was able to do so while seriously ill, and while evading detection as the foreign office sent

---

22   Samuel Richards' travels and activities during 1854–56, including his first notation of correspondence with Jane Mayer in 1855 and the brief description of their early 1856 wedding, may be tracked or inferred from his journal entries for this period. See Samuel W. Richards Papers, Church History Library.

This 1863 signed portrait of Henrietta Polydore was drawn by her cousin, Dante Gabriel Rossetti (1828–1882), a famed English poet, illustrator, translator, and painter, who was one of the co-founders of the Pre-Raphaelite Brotherhood in 1848. *Courtesy of Victoria and Albert Museum, London.*

the diplomatic equivalent of wanted posters to British consuls in American ports, was a remarkable display of her resourcefulness, resilience, and determination. Upon reaching England in 1856, Henrietta Mayer Polydore described her trek across the "Great American Desert" in vivid terms that stuck in the minds of her Rossetti in-laws who heard her account of this adventure. William Michael Rossetti journalized, "She has gone through any number of singular adventures. At one time she was near being exchanged to an Indian for a horse, as his squaw, and she actually some years ago, on hearing of her Father's illness or distress, came from Salt Lake to Liverpool, having in her pocket at starting only three dollars, and not spending any of it on the way."[23]

By the beginning of 1857 Henrietta, accompanied by her family, was back in New Orleans hoping to move to Utah during the summer, but their near-destitution, the precarious state of

---

23   Jan Marsh, *Christina Rossetti, A Literary Biography* (London: Pimlico, 1995), 363, quoted in Jill Waller, "Christina Rossetti's Cheltenham Connection," *Cheltenham Local History Society—Journal*, 18 (2002): 73.

Mr. Mayer's health, and the onset of the Utah War in the spring forced them all to remain in Louisiana.[24]

If the sequencing and arrangements of travel for the Mayer family is confusing, what is clear is that from mid-decade young Henrietta lived apart from her mother in the care of aunt Jane Mayer in the Salt Lake City home of Elder Richards. She did so under the alias "Lucy," although within the family Samuel Richards used Henrietta's longstanding nickname "Lalla." It was a remote and secretive living arrangement presumably designed to throw a distraught Henry Polydore off the trail of his missing daughter. Consistent with this obfuscation but counter to church records, Jane would later deny in U.S. district court that she and Samuel had married, so from outward appearances there was no overt linkage between the surnames Richards and Mayer by which Jane and her niece could be traced to Salt Lake.

During 1857 the Mayer family, including Henrietta Mayer Polydore, removed from Louisiana not to Utah but to Arkansas, where they became cotton farmers, an occupation closely linked to the British textile industry, through the port of New Orleans. Although members of the Rossetti family maintained friendly relations with Mrs. Polydore as best they could long-distance, the years-long separation of mother and daughter prompted some of the Rossettis to question the quality of the mother's parenting. Mrs. Polydore tried to maintain contact with little Henrietta, writing to her in early 1857 that "nothing will prevent my coming in the summer if you do not come to us. I hope you have learned a great deal since I left. I think we shall never be separated again. When we do meet it will be the happiest time I have known for

---

24   Henrietta Mayer Polydore's extensive travel and herculean efforts to relocate her family from England during 1856 are described in Henrietta Cheek Mayer (New Orleans) to Jane Mayer Richards and "Lalla" (Salt Lake City), January 20, 1857, Jane Mayer Richards Papers, Church History Library.

years. . . . I cannot describe the anxiety I am in about you." In the same letter, Mrs. Polydore added a postscript for Jane: "Write some at once. I am full of anxiety about the child as you may well suppose."[25] Dashing these hopes was the onset of the Utah War in the spring of 1857 and its disruption of travel across the plains and Rockies.

How young Henrietta experienced the war in Salt Lake City in the midst of a household that included several sister wives (Samuel married again in March 1857) and nearly twenty children is one of the intriguing parts of her story for which there is no record. Also unknown is the way in which Jane Mayer Richards and Henrietta interacted during this period with another fugitive member of the extended Richards family whose dramatic flight to Salt Lake City from Europe with a young son paralleled their own story. We refer to the case of Josephine Marie Augustine de la Harpe Ludert, a Russian countess of Swiss parentage who converted to Mormonism, abandoned her husband (the Russian consul general in Havana), and in 1856 fled to Utah via Switzerland with her nine-year-old son, Joseph. She did so a step ahead of the tsarist government's attempts to prevent her departure from Europe, and crossed the Great Plains with a Swiss handcart company a few months ahead of the Willie-Martin disaster. In March 1857 Josephine became the plural wife of Apostle Franklin D. Richards, Samuel's brother. Because of their family connection and commonalities in their personal experiences, Josephine, Jane, and their two children presumably socialized in Salt Lake City's Fourteenth Ward during the Utah War, but there is no documentary support for such intriguing speculation.[26]

---

25   Henrietta Mayer Polydore to Henrietta Polydore and Jane Mayer Richards, early 1857, Jane Mayer Richards, Correspondence, Church History Library.

26   Ardis E. Parshall, "Josephine Marie Augustine de la Harpe Ludert Ursenbach: From the Tsar's Court to the Kingdom of God," blog essay, June 3, 2009, Keepapitchinin.com, accessed November 8, 2020.

ELDER SAMUEL W. RICHARDS (1824–1909), PRESIDENT OF THE LATTER-DAY SAINT BRITISH MISSION AND HENRIETTA'S PROTECTOR IN UTAH Member of a prominent, influential Utah family, he was sketched in 1854 by Frederick Piercy at about the time he met Henrietta's aunt Jane Mayer, later his fourth wife. *Used by permission, Utah State Historical Society.*

What is known, though, is that in the late summer of 1857, as the Utah Expedition marched across Nebraska Territory toward the Continental Divide, Brigham Young abruptly called the head of her new family, Samuel W. Richards, to resume leadership of the British Mission on an emergency basis and, en route to Liverpool, to brief Thomas L. Kane of Philadelphia, Young's closest and most influential non-Mormon friend, about his plans for the defense of Utah. An account of how Elder Richards conducted this clandestine mission and then returned from Great Britain to Utah in May 1858 in the midst of the Latter-day Saints' Move South—treks that involved two passages through army lines—is available elsewhere.[27]

Suffice it to say here that, although it is not known what economic and practical support Richards provided his family in his absence, he did try to sustain a quasi-parental relationship with Henrietta on an emotional basis via messages for her in his letters

---

27   MacKinnon, ed., *At Sword's Point, Part 1*, 252–54, 406–409. For additional information about the Move South, see pages 154–55.

to wife Jane. For example, from New York on September 18, 1857, he attempted to convey to "Lucy" what he considered to be the blessings of life among the Latter-day Saints (including polygamy) for young women compared to the sordid conditions he saw in the cities of the American Atlantic seaboard, and, by inference, his dread of the impact on Latter-day Saint society if the army occupied the Salt Lake Valley. (Ironically, Richards' fears were what today would be called the flip side of Henry F. Polydore's concerns if his daughter, whatever her location, remained in Utah society as she approached marriageable age.) In the same letter, Richards admonished Jane to "take good care of Lucy (or Henrietta) and be a Mother to her, and to our darling little Phineas. Lucy should have every reasonable opportunity at a good school with the children. . . . God bless you, the *baby* and Lucy." Two months later, as the Utah Expedition went into winter quarters at Fort Bridger 113 miles from Salt Lake City, Samuel wrote to Jane from Liverpool, "I hope you will be able to make Henrietta feel quite comfortable with you, & Mary and you will be able to furnish her with such things as may be necessary to fit her for going to school &c. &c. as I would not like the education of the children neglected either at home or elsewhere. I want her to feel quite at home & comfortable."[28]

---

28 Samuel W. Richards to Jane Mayer Richards, September 18 and November 20, 1857, both Samuel Whitney Richards Papers, Church History Library. Probably fearing interception of his letters, as many Latter-day Saint leaders did, Richards often referred to Henrietta by her alias ("Lucy") or nickname ("Lalla") rather than by her given name. Interestingly, coming as it did in the midst of the Utah War, Richards told Jane on September 18 immediately after trying to brief Kane, "I am happy in my Mission, which is indeed an important one, and one which has a great effect upon the Saints, and its results will be mighty upon the World."

This undated (but almost certainly post–Civil War) photo of Albert Gallatin Browne, Jr. was taken at the studio of James Wallace Black in Boston. *Courtesy of Browne family descendant Katherine Greenough.*

Robert Carter (1819–1879), the editor-mentor who engineered Browne's appointment in 1857 as the New York Tribune's Utah War correspondent. *Sketch by Jacques Reich for Appleton's Cyclopaedia of American Biography (1900).*

Why Browne Wrote
The Ward of the Three Guardians

BEFORE TURNING TO THE TEXT OF BROWNE'S novella, it is important to understand why he wrote as he did in 1877. Unfortunately, the author provided no direct insight into his creative impulses at that time, but an immersion for sixty years in Browne's personal papers prompts us to speculate about several possible explanations. We do so mindful of historian Gary Topping's recent encouragement for historians, especially those engaged in Utah studies, "to use evidence to read between the lines and, in so doing, offer greater interpretive insight than would otherwise be available . . . Taking this approach can offer interpretive possibilities into the motives and inner drive of historical actors. . . . Historians are going to have to learn to be content with doing part of our work in the shadowy world of conjecture, possibility, probability, and interpretation based on reading-between-the-lines evidence."[1]

First, we note that Browne had a dramatic Utah story to tell that had been "marinating" untold for twenty years. It was the tale of one of the great adventures of his life—his arduous crossing of

---

1   Gary Topping, "The History Between the Lines," *Utah Historical Quarterly* 88 (Summer 2020): 228–29, 233.

the Rockies and Great Plains in the dead of winter during January–March 1858 to carry dispatches from Fort Bridger to army headquarters in New York and the Buchanan administration in Washington. For all that Browne wrote about the Utah War for publication in the *Tribune* during 1857–58, none of it dealt with his most personal experiences, including his virtually unknown west-to-east winter trek and subsequent return to the army in the spring. Publishing *The Ward of the Three Guardians* under his own name, and doing so during 1877 in perhaps the most prestigious journal of literature and opinion in the English-speaking world, enabled him to break through the culturally enforced inhibitions of an earlier era. It was a way of shedding the anonymity of his monthly dispatches from the field to the *Tribune* and the soon-to-follow, three-part essay of 1859 for *The Atlantic Monthly*.[2] By combining this material with the related, equally unexploited story of young Henrietta Polydore's travails, Browne was able to create a non-fiction novel loaded with the dramatic Latter-day Saint, western, and English elements irresistible to Victorian readers on both sides of the Atlantic. It was the rich vein of material also mined by Arthur Conan Doyle ten years later when he

---

2   The restrictions on novelists' and reporters' self-identification and use of other people's names in their work is explained in Kathryn Whitford, "The Young Officer Who Rode Beside Me: An Examination of Nineteenth-Century Naming Conventions," *American Studies* 23 (Spring 1982): 5–22. When Browne's widow prepared a biographical sketch of him for a Harvard reunion, she unfortunately included no reference to *Ward* in the exhaustive list of his other publications. This omission reinforced the longstanding anonymity surrounding Browne's Utah experiences, an anonymity we believe *Ward* was, in part, intended to remedy. See Mattie Griffith Browne memorandum in Albert G. Browne, Jr. File, Records of the Class of 1853 Secretary, HUD 253.505, Box 62. Among the earliest identifications of Browne's newspaper role in Utah took place during his return trip home after the war, when he stopped in St. Louis to pay a courtesy call on the editor of the *Democrat*. As a result, that newspaper described him in its November 16, 1858, issue as "the Utah correspondent of the New York Tribune."

brought out *A Study in Scarlet* to describe the perils of a young girl among the Latter-day Saints and a series of fictive murders spilling from the deserts of Utah into fog-shrouded London.

But why did Browne do so in June 1877? Aside from the influence of the sheer passage of time since his Utah experiences, we believe that this was a time when Albert G. Browne, Jr. was cultivating a more public persona than had theretofore been the case. He was working as an editor of the *Evening Post* in Manhattan and emerging from a long, successful public campaign to bring down the very embodiment of American political corruption, William Marcy ("Boss") Tweed, former mayor of Manhattan and leader of the Democratic Party's Tammany Hall political machine. In November 1875 *Harper's Weekly* published his high-profile expose about Tweed and his sordid machinations with members of New York State's legislature and courts that was influential in the campaign against Tweed.[3] As a result, there was public speculation that Browne was under consideration for appointment as legal reporter for the U.S. Supreme Court, a prestigious role similar to one he had played in the Massachusetts court system during 1867–69. Browne did not go to Washington, but almost immediately after the appearance of his *Harper's Weekly* expose, Albert moved to an editor's position at the *New York Herald*, the highest-circulation newspaper in the country. When Boston newspaperman and friend Charles Hale (Harvard Class of 1850) published a series of articles in *The Atlantic Monthly* during 1876–77 about his experiences as U.S. consul-general in Egypt,

---

3   Albert G. Browne, Jr., "The Combined Rings: A Searching Criticism of the Decisions of the New York Court of Appeals in the City [Tweed] and Canal Ring Suits," special supplement to *Harper's Weekly*, November 13, 1875.

this example may have stimulated Albert's own urges to write more about Utah.[4]

Simply put, in the quite different *milieu* of New York in the mid-1870s, Browne may have been more comfortable with a higher profile than in his earlier, more self-effacing Boston years of the late 1850s. Writing a novella under his own name would have been consistent with such a change in his attitude about name recognition.

Even more important was the fact that in 1877 Utah and Mormonism were very much in the news, and the public was ravenous for more. That year John D. Lee, Brigham Young's religiously adopted son, was executed by firing squad for his role in the Mountain Meadows massacre of 1857; a few months later Young himself died of natural but undetermined causes in Salt Lake City at age seventy-six. Editorial and printing lead times for *The Atlantic Monthly* were such that Lee's execution in March 1877 was not a stimulus for Browne's novella (published in June, less than three months later), but the extensive publicity accompanying the hunt for Lee, his capture, and the two trials that led to his conviction kept Utah on Browne's mind for more than five years as he wrestled with creating something like *Ward* and then actually wrote it. If one scans the New York dailies for the several weeks preceding and following *Ward*'s appearance in late May, they are loaded with sensational material from Utah describing sex, violence, and endless conspiracies—all contributed by stringers or paid correspondents sent out from Manhattan as Browne had been in 1857. Supplementing these reports from the West were titillating dispatches from throughout the country describing the

---

4   Charles Hale, "The Khedive and the Court," *The Atlantic Monthly* 37 (May 1876): 513–20, and "Consular Service and Society in Egypt," *The Atlantic Monthly* 40 (September 1877): 280–90.

"Situation of the Mormons in Utah,"
editorial cartoon in San Francisco's *Wasp* magazine
This depiction of the jousting between a demonized Brigham Young and the armed might of the U.S. government over polygamy reflects the over-heated atmosphere of the Reconstruction era in which Browne wrote *Ward*. *George Frederick Keller cartoon (1879) in public domain.*

national lecture tour of Ann Eliza Young, the polygamous wife who left Brigham Young and then sued him for divorce.[5]

Also bubbling at the time was the legal appeal of the conviction of George Reynolds, one of Brigham Young's office clerks, for violation of the 1862 Morrill Anti-Bigamy Act. It was a "test" case that in 1877 was wending its way through the judicial minefield between the supreme courts of Utah Territory and the United

5   Typical of such sensational coverage of Utah affairs were, among others, the *New York Herald*'s issues of May 20, and June 2 and 16, 1877.

States. Reynolds' fate was being adjudicated just as the federal government began to use the anti-polygamy tools provided by the even more draconian Poland Act of 1874.[6] It was also a time during which Congress was debating the wisdom of resolving the country's enduring "Mormon problem" by totally dismembering Utah Territory or continuing to reduce the size of its borders piecemeal, as had already been done six times during the 1860s.[7] If post-war Reconstruction ended with the withdrawal of the U.S. Army from the eleven states of the Confederacy in 1876–77, it was a time when President Ulysses S. Grant declared his intent to turn his attention to polygamous, autocratic Utah Territory with the same ferocity and tactics he had used in the South.

Finally, there is the fact that in 1877 Henrietta Polydore was dead, having passed away less than three years earlier during one of her episodic returns to the United States to visit her mother in coastal Mississippi. Her passing removed vestiges of any social and literary barriers inhibiting Browne from writing about her adventures, although, as discussed in a subsequent chapter, there is a distinct possibility that he was unaware of Henrietta's passing or even the story of her later life as it had unfolded after returning to England at year-end 1858.

---

6   Edward Brown Firmage and Richard Collin Mangrum, *Zion in the Courts: A Legal History of the Church of Jesus Christ of Latter-day Saints, 1830–1900* (Urbana and Chicago: University of Illinois Press, 1988).

7   W. Paul Reeve, "Reconstruction, Religion, and the West: The Great Impeacher Meets the Mormons," *Journal of Mormon History* 46 (April 2020): 5–45; MacKinnon, "'Like Splitting a Man Up His Backbone': The Territorial Dismemberment of Utah, 1850–1896," *Utah Historical Quarterly* 71 (Spring 2003): 100–24.

PART TWO

The Novella:
The Ward of the Three Guardians

So to what extent is [the book] "true"? . . . the premise and central characters of the novel were clearly rooted in reality, but what of the narrative? . . . What matters is not whether [the book] is "true," but whether it is any good. The real measure of "truth" in any novel is not whether the characters, places and events portrayed exist beyond the pages of the book, but, rather, whether they seem authentic to us as readers.

GRAEME MACRAE BURNET,
THE ACCIDENT ON THE A35

An explanation of novella pseudonyms

IN THE NOVELLA . . .	IN ACTUALITY . . .
Henrietta Perego	Henrietta Polydore
Mrs. Perego	Henrietta Mayer Polydore
Julian Perego	Henry Polydore
Jane Moore Peckham	Jane Mayer Richards
Sam Peckham	Samuel W. Richards
The General	Brevet Brig. Gen. Albert Sidney Johnston
The Doctor	Albert G. Browne, Jr.
The Judge	Delana R. Eckels
The Marshal	Peter K. Dotson
The Attorney	Washington J. McCormick
The Guide	John Mills Hockaday
The Lieutenant or Aide	1st Lt. Lawrence A. Williams
Elder Josiah Baxter, the Landlord	Edward Cuthbert
Captain John, the Quartermaster	Captain John H. Dickerson
Indian Tom	Mary Tecumbiats
The Lieutenant-Colonel	Brevet Lt. Col. Edward R. S. Canby
The Lieutenant-Colonel's Wife	Louisa Hawkins Canby
Jo Brooks	W. J. Brooks
St. Albans, Hertfordshire	Cheltenham, Gloucestershire, England

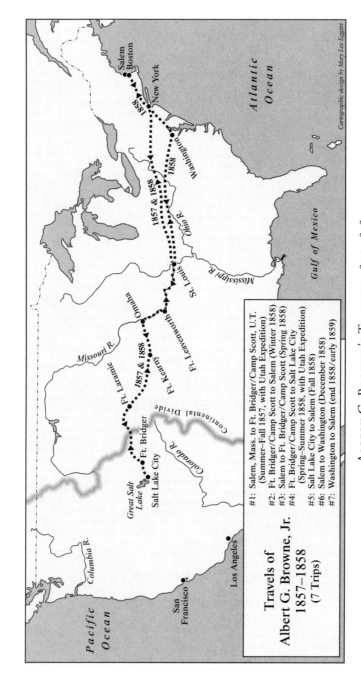

Travels of
Albert G. Browne, Jr.
1857–1858
(7 Trips)

#1: Salem, Mass. to Ft. Bridger/Camp Scott, U.T.
   (Summer–Fall 1857, with Utah Expedition)
#2: Ft. Bridger/Camp Scott to Salem (Winter 1858)
#3: Salem to Ft. Bridger/Camp Scott (Spring 1858)
#4: Ft. Bridger/Camp Scott to Salt Lake City
   (Spring–Summer 1858, with Utah Expedition)
#5: Salt Lake City to Salem (Fall 1858)
#6: Salem to Washington (December 1858)
#7: Washington to Salem (end 1858/early 1859)

ALBERT G. BROWNE'S TRAVELS, 1857–1858

Map commissioned by authors; cartographer Mary Lee Eggart of Baton Rouge.

"In the Saddle by Starlight"

ALBERT BROWNE HEADS EAST,
HENRIETTA POLYDORE FLEES WEST

⚜ EDITORIAL NOTES

As throughout Albert G. Browne Jr.'s novella, this opening section described accurately what he experienced first-hand but then shifted to fiction in order to present matters of which the author had little or no direct knowledge.[1] His descriptions of Camp Scott and Fort Bridger are examples of the former. Browne wrote them in 1877 after consulting his scrapbook of newspaper clippings, especially the dispatch he sent to the Tribune on November 26, 1857.[2] An example of the latter is his substitution of the names "Sam Peckham" and "Jane Moore" for

---

1   Portions of this section may be found in MacKinnon, ed., *At Sword's Point, Part 2,* 96–100.

2   Browne's scrapbook may be found in Special Collections, Call No. x F826.N49, J. Willard Marriott Library, University of Utah, Salt Lake City; photocopy in MacKinnon's research files. This volume, Browne's principal research tool other than his memory, is described in Jonathan Frederick Bingham, "On Jon's Desk: Scrapbook of Clippings from New York Daily Tribune, a collection of newspaper clippings concerning the Utah War (1850s)," blog entry February 28, 2017, "Open Book—News from the Rare Books Department of Special Collections at the J. Willard Marriott Library, University of Utah, " found at: openbook.lib.utah.edu, accessed August 21, 2020. First use of this document was for MacKinnon, ed., *At Sword's Point, Part 1.*

Samuel W. Richards and Jane Elizabeth Mayer. The editors believe that "Peckham" may have been inspired by the name of Wheeler Hazard Peckham, a special prosecutor for the State of New York whom Browne encountered in Manhattan during the mid-1870s. Use of "Moore" was perhaps prompted by Browne's interactions at Camp Scott with Asst. Surgeon John Moore, regimental medical officer for the Fifth U.S. Infantry. Richards was not a member of the Quorum of the Twelve Apostles, as Jim Bridger asserts here, but he was a senior leader just below that level. Bridger may never have met either Samuel or Jane, and Browne would have done so no earlier than August 1858 in Salt Lake City.

This section's most significant departure from the facts came at its opening, with Browne's invention of a New Year's Day reception in General Johnston's hospital tent. It was an event that never happened because of the shortage of ingredients necessary to stage such a meal and Johnston's insistence that he draw only the reduced rations issued to his troops.[3] An examination of the diaries of the officers most likely to be invited to any such New Year's gathering—Maj. Fitz John Porter (Johnston's adjutant and tent mate), Capt. John W. Phelps, and Capt. Jesse A. Gove—yields no description of such a reception.

3　Two weeks before this fictive New Year's Day "feast" Johnston wrote to a relative in Louisville: "I said we have abundance, but inasmuch as no one, from the Governor and civil officers to the private soldier, can obtain more than one ration, we have nothing to give in the way of hospitality. The day before the reduction [in rations] took place, we gave a dinner to the Governor, Chief Justice, &c, on our surplus in the larder. Since then I do not think we could feed an extra rat at our mess, such is our health and so nicely is the quality allowed adjusted to the measure of our wants." Johnston to unidentified relative, December 12, 1857, unidentified newspaper clipping, February 16, 1858, Phelps Scrapbook, New York Public Library. Elaborate meals provided by the officers of the Tenth Infantry and Mrs. Gov. Cumming on New Year's Eve and Day, respectively, are described in "Life at Camp Scott— How the Holidays Were Spent," Dispatch, "A.B.C." [David A. Burr], January 4, 1858, New York Times, April 9, 1858.

Clearly Johnston broached the subject of a courier mission east to Browne very early in January, but he did so under circumstances far more basic than those described in Ward. *The mission itself was necessitated by the intelligence Johnston received at year-end from returned prisoners of war. The selection of Browne rather than a soldier to act as courier was counter-intuitive and mysterious. The editors believe Johnston approached Browne because he needed a well-educated, articulate messenger capable of interacting effectively with General Scott and perhaps even President Buchanan. All of the Utah Expedition's junior officers were troop commanders badly needed in their under-officered regiments; they could not be spared, and their senior sergeants were either likewise essential or lacked the requisite polish for high-level consultations in New York and Washington. Johnston liked to surround himself with high-status younger men; he would have been pre-disposed to send Browne (or someone like him) even though a civilian. In short, A. G. Browne, Jr. was qualified, available, willing, and expendable.*

In an October letter, Albert had written his father to report that he and Johnston first met shortly after their separate detachments joined forces at the Sweetwater River. The implication was that the two men had bonded, and Browne confided to his father he expected "to act as aid[e] to Col. Johns[t]on." Although army regulations did not provide for such an appointment, there was nothing to bar Johnston from seeking Browne's help on an informal basis, and he did so in early January. That Browne was in a position to provide Johnston with ongoing newspaper publicity only added to his attractiveness.[4]

Jim Bridger's description in this section of his encounter in 1854 with "Jane Moore" and eight-year-old "Henerietta" as part of a Mormon

---

4   Albert G. Browne, Jr. to Albert G. Browne, Sr., ca. October 18, 1857, described in Browne, Sr. to Mary Ellen ("Nellie") Browne, December 11, 1857, Browne Family Papers, MC 298, Folder 5, Schlesinger Library. Albert wrote from near Pacific Springs just west of South Pass.

handcart company was also pure fiction in several ways. First, as discussed above, the small Polydore-Mayer party traveled from the Missouri River to the Salt Lake Valley in 1855, not a year earlier. Second, Brigham Young did not introduce handcarts into the Mormon cross-plains transportation arrangements until the summer of 1856. And finally, at the time Browne placed Jim at his fort as witness to a Mormon crossing of Blacks Fork, "Old Gabriel" was back at his farm in Missouri. He had been driven out of Fort Bridger by a Mormon posse during the summer of 1853 and did not return until November 1857 as chief scout for Albert Sidney Johnston's Utah Expedition.

ON THE AFTERNOON OF NEW YEAR'S DAY IN 1858, the medley of troops, teamsters, and adventurers who composed what was called the Utah Expedition lay huddled in a dreary camp, seven thousand feet above the level of the sea, in the shallow valley of Black's Fork, a few miles south of a little stone redoubt named Fort Bridger, which is still visible from the track of the Pacific railroad.[3] They had marched from the frontier of Missouri in June [July], confident of entering the Salt Lake Valley before the first bleak storms of the autumn. But the Mormons rose in arms, fortified the canyons which were the avenues to their capital, harassed the army by burning wagon trains and stampeding the quartermaster's cattle, and finally arrested its march in this desolate spot, a hundred and fifty miles east of the Salt Lake, from which it was separated by the massive and

---

3   Established in 1843, Fort Bridger was a civilian trading post to service emigrant traffic. The area served as a crossroads for many routes, including the Mormon Trail. Fred R. Gowans and Eugene E. Campbell, *Fort Bridger: Island in the Wilderness* (Provo, Ut.: Brigham Young University Press, 1975). The U.P.R.R. had been built through that area during 1868–69.

snow-bound barrier of the Wasatch Mountains.[6] Between bluffs three or four hundred feet high the river [Blacks Fork] murmured down to the fort under a sheet of ice, and ran zig-zag along a strip of bottom-land half a mile wide, which was clad in unbroken snow save in the bends of the stream, where it was dotted with log-huts and tents, from whose chimneys a hundred thin ribbons of smoke floated quietly up into the sky. Among them rose a tall flag-staff, shaped from a mountain pine, on which a starred-and-striped ensign was flapping in the frosty air. A few shivering willow bushes and cottonwoods, despoiled of foliage and charred by fires set by the Mormons, lined the edges of the fork, but no evergreens softened the glare of the landscape, and, besides the streamers of smoke, not a sign of life was visible, except on the flat tops of the bluffs where sentinels were pacing.

Inside of a wide-spreading hospital-tent, which was pitched near the centre of the camp and loomed conspicuously above its neighbors, there was a gathering, this dreary afternoon, whose gayety was in merry contrast with the savage and sombre scenery without. The officers had conspired with the only lady who was sharing the discomforts of the campaign—the wife of the lieutenant-colonel of one of the infantry regiments—to celebrate the day with the best approach Camp Scott could make to the New Year's usages of the Fifth Avenue. The lieutenant-colonel's wife was an older campaigner than most of the conspirators. In fever-hospitals at Vera Cruz, in tangled ambushes among the Everglades, and in all the perils of frontier service, she had followed her husband for twenty years, with a fortitude that rendered her ingenious in the

---

6   "The Wasatch Mountains extend in a north-south orientation approximately 160 miles from southern Idaho to central Utah. The range forms part of the eastern boundary of the Great Basin and the western edge of the Rocky Mountains." Van Cott, *Utah Place Names*, 390. Latter-day Saint assertions that harassment by the Nauvoo Legion forced the Utah Expedition into winter quarters overlook the decisive impact of winter weather on the army's ability to move west of Fort Bridger.

expedients of military life.[7] So in a hospitable chimney built of timber and clay at one end of the tent a huge fire was devouring half a cord of logs; the floor of the pavilion was laid with planks from dismantled wagons; and on a long table built of the same material, and covered with strips of gaudy calico provided by the sutler[8] for the Salt Lake market, there were the remnants of a feast, the masterpiece of which was a monstrous pie, secretly composed by the general's aide from dried apples and dough, with some hair oil that had been discovered among the sutler's stores. Butter for many a month had been a thing only of memory and of hope. So [too] with lard. So also with all fresh fruits and vegetables. The wagon trains which the Mormons intercepted and burned two months before contained almost all the bacon that belonged to the army rations, and four thousand men were struggling to survive the winter of an Esquimau [Eskimo] without the aid of his usual [fatty] diet. So familiar had the situation become that the disclosure of the composition of the pie crust caused not a qualm in the most delicate stripling who partook of it.

It was during the burst of laughter which greeted the revelation of the secret of the pastry that the general, tapping my shoulder, drew me aside into a corner of the tent, and startled me with the whisper, "Would you like to go to church on Easter in New

---

7   Browne describes Louisa Hawkins Canby, wife of the Tenth Infantry's Brevet Lt. Col. E.R.S. Canby. For an anonymous adulatory post–Civil War remembrance of Mrs. Canby's hospital work at Camp Scott, see "Gen. Canby," *Daily Sentinel* (Raleigh, N.C.), September 11, 1867. She was not the only officer's wife accompanying the Utah Expedition—there were four others—and there were also female company laundresses at the garrison, many of whom were married to enlistees although not recognized by men like Browne and Capt. Marcy in their newspaper dispatches as "ladies."

8   Sutlers were civilian camp followers licensed by the army to sell a wide variety of provisions and goods to the troops. Each of the Utah Expedition's regiments had one. During the Mexican War, Governor Cumming was a sutler, which did not help his image ten years later at Camp Scott.

York?"[9] I think it must have been a minute before I replied; for something in his manner satisfied me that he was not joking, and set my fancy wandering off across a thousand miles of snowy desert, and then floating down the Missouri River, steaming [by train] across the land a thousand miles further, and arriving at Trinity Church on a sparkling morning of the early spring, when the yellow buds of the willows were swelling in the grave-yard, and a battalion of pretty girls, with dainty new bonnets, was pressing through the portal to the music of organ and orchestra and chanting children's voices.

Five days afterwards I had finished my preparations for the long and perilous winter journey to "the States."[10] Half a dozen men, selected for my companions and escort, were sworn to secrecy as to even the fact of the adventure; and its purpose was only communicated to me in confidence, lest some accident might befall the dispatches which I was to bear. The situation was indeed serious. A private inspection of the commissary stores had convinced the general that they were insufficient to subsist the army till military operations could be resumed against the Mormons; the dispatches contained an earnest appeal to General Scott to force a convoy of provisions through to the camp; and I was warned that the fortunes of the campaign would largely depend upon the safety and speed of my journey.

It was a dark and dismal evening[11] when I raked the ashes over the embers of my camp fire, tied up the door of my tent, and crossed the ice at the bend of the creek to take supper with the

---

9   The significance of New York, rather than Browne's Salem home, was that it was the army's headquarters.

10   Settlers and travelers in U.S. territories generally referred to the rest of the country as "the States."

11   Unwittingly, or otherwise, Browne began this sentence with the then-famous (but now ridiculed) opening phrase of Edward George Bulwer-Lytton's 1830 novel *Paul Clifford*: "It was a dark and stormy night."

general and get my last instructions. I was to set out before dawn
the next morning, and, for fear of outlying parties of Mormons,
instead of striking due east was to travel south along Green River
to the mouth of Bitter Creek,[12] follow that up as far as the snow
would permit, and then journey northeast, by the compass, across
the table-land towards the Wind River Mountains,[13] till I should
reach the Sweetwater and the Oregon trail that leads through the
South Pass. At the general's table I found the famous old trapper,
Jim Bridger, who had been summoned there to give me information about the route.

Bridger was a marvelous and interesting character. In physical
appearance a counterpart of Cooper's Leatherstocking,[14] he was
unbent by age, without a morsel of superfluous flesh, and lithe and
sinewy as a willow wand, with a skin as brown and wrinkled as
parchment shriveled by heat. For almost fifty years he had trapped
and hunted in these boundless western wilds, from the Red River
of the North to the Staked Plains of Texas.[15] He gazed upon the
expanse of the Great Salt Lake a generation before Frémont trod
the shore.[16] Even as early as 1830, so he often asserted, he had seen

---

12   In ascending Bitter Creek from its confluence with the Green River, Browne's party
     would have been traveling north-northeast toward the South Pass roughly parallel-
     ing the route of today's U.P.R.R. and Interstate 80.

13   The Wind River Mountains are part of the Rocky Mountains in western Wyoming.

14   The *Leatherstocking Tales*, written by American author James Fenimore Cooper,
     were a series of five popular novels set in the north woods of eighteenth-century
     New York that outline the exploits of Natty Bumppo, a Daniel Boone–like charac-
     ter—similar in many ways to Jim Bridger.

15   The Red River flows northerly from Minnesota and North Dakota to Lake Winni-
     peg in Canada. The Staked Plains, a high flat land in what is now northwest Texas
     and northeast New Mexico, is one of the largest most arid tablelands on the conti-
     nent (https://tshaonline.org/handbook/online/articles/ryl02).

16   Western explorer, John C. Fremont (who became the newly formed Republican Par-
     ty's first presidential nominee in 1856), arrived at the Great Salt Lake in 1844 and
     named one of its principal islands for himself. Although in 1856 Fremont campaigned
     on an anti-polygamy presidential platform, he was grateful for aid Latter-day Saints

the wonders of the Fire River Valley, a tale which we were fond of inciting him to tell, and to which we listened with a steadfast incredulity that reached its climax when the old man, after a description of the head waters of the Yellowstone as abounding in orange groves and crocodiles, insisted that the ground spit fire at every step and spouted forth geysers three hundred feet high. Peace to his prevaricating soul! We know today that what we esteemed his most monstrous lie was seasoned with truth.[17]

One of Bridger's aggressive traits was a fanatical faith that everything loveliest in the world was to be found somewhere between Kansas City on the one side and Sacramento on the other.[18] The fascinating feature of the general's supper consisted of a course of beef sausages, which were manufactured by an ingenious machine that had just been constructed by a corporal who was detailed for duty as a carpenter. This machine was the envy and the despair of every inhabitant of the camp who had tasted of its products, for the daily diet at all the other mess-tables had now for many weeks consisted of steaks and joints from the tough cattle of the quarter-master's trains, which tasked the strongest jaws and the most resolute digestion. Bridger honestly regarded the device of this machine as worth in itself the whole cost and peril of the Utah Expedition.[19] He would sit by the hour watching its operations with the immobile interest of an Indian. I doubt whether he ever had heard of the Jacquard loom, or of

gave his expedition in 1853. Tom Chaffin, *Pathfinder: John Charles Frémont and the Course of American Empire* (Norman: University of Oklahoma Press, 2014).

17 For additional information about Jim Bridger's storied life, see J. Cecil Alter, *Jim Bridger*, rev. ed. (Norman: University of Oklahoma Press, 1979), and Jerry Enzler, *Jim Bridger: Trailblazer of the American West* (Norman: University of Oklahoma Press, 2021).

18 In 1858, what later became "Kansas City" was called "Westport Landing" on the Missouri River.

19 There was no such machine in use at the Utah Expedition's winter quarters and no Corporal Jenkins as its inventor.

Maj. James Felix "Old Gabriel"
Bridger (1804–1881),
Utah Expedition's chief guide
Exercising a novelist's license, Browne assigned
his Jim Bridger character to narrate a fictive
description of young "Henerietta Perego" and
her aunt "Jane Moore" in-transit across the
plains to Utah. *Photo courtesy Wikimedia.*

Erastus Bigelow's carpet-weaving machine;[20] but, even if he had,
he would have rated those inventions far inferior in genius and
benevolence to Corporal Jenkins' sausage-mill. Accordingly this
evening, when the table was cleared and we were gathered around
the fire, Bridger, with a tin mug of apple-jack compounded of
whisky and dried apples in one hand, and a pipe stuffed with
Lynchburg tobacco in the other, waxed eloquent over the com-
forts of the camp.[21]

"My last words to you, doctor," said he, addressing me by name,
with an old German title which some of my acquaintances had
discovered and imported to the camp, "are, remember these

---

20   The Jacquard loom used a series of punched card to mechanically enable weavers
to create intricate lace and other woven designs. *Encyclopedia Britannica.* Erastus
Bigelow invented the power loom in 1837, a carpet-weaving machine, which made
lace and many types of carpet. Chaim M. Rosenberg, *The Great Workshop: Boston's
Victorian Age* (Charleston, S.C.: Arcadia Publishing, 2004), 69.

21   Apple jack was a high-alcohol cider made from fermented apples. Lynchburg, Virginia "had become the largest loose-leaf tobacco market in the world." https://www
.newsadvance.com/news/local/from-the-archives-when-tobacco-was-king/
collection_51689c62-5d70-11e6-b53f-3b8ef6b60e56.html.

1ST LT. LAWRENCE A. WILLIAMS
(1833–1879), 10TH U.S. INFANTRY,
AIDE DE CAMP TO GEN. ALBERT
SIDNEY JOHNSTON
As a relative of Virginia's Lees and
Washingtons, he was typical of the well-
connected southern West Pointers with whom
Johnston surrounded himself in Utah. *Camp
Floyd, Utah photo (1859) by Mills & Jagiello,
courtesy Ephriam D. Dickson III and National
Archives.*

sassingers when you get to [New] York city.[22] You won't find their equal in the States, if you s'arch for it from Council Bluffs to Novy Scoshy. What more on airth can a man hanker for this winter, lieutenant?" he added, diverting his conversation to the general's aide, who also was sipping apple-jack in a corner of the fireplace.

Now the general's aide was a handsome young officer who was chafing visibly under the privations of the campaign, and more than once during the autumn had expressed a wish to be plastered with postage stamps and sent East in a mailbag, if he could escape in no other way.[23] "If you mean me, Uncle Jim," he said quickly,

---

22 "Doctor" was a reference to Browne's Ph.D. degree from Heidelberg University of which readers were unaware. "Sassingers" were Jim Bridger–speak for "sausages."

23 The unnamed lieutenant was 1st Lt. Lawrence A. Williams of the Tenth Infantry's Co. G. He was a cousin to Robert E. Lee's wife, Mary, a descendant of Martha Washington. He was an example of Johnston's fondness for able, politically, or socially connected West Pointers. Williams did not become Johnston's aide until April 1858 when he became a brigadier. Browne appropriated the mail bag/postage stamp story from legends circulating among bored officers at posts all along the Oregon Trail. Williams, West Point Class of 1852 [Cullum #1571], was dismissed from the Army during the Civil War after he went absent without leave to visit Mary Lee in Virginia, a huge blunder in view of her husband's role in the Confederate army.

"I think it's an infernal shame for the United States to keep a fellow here for six months knee-deep in the snow, with no women in camp except the lieutenant-colonel's wife. I don't count for anything the six sergeants' wives who do washing. The sausages are pretty good, but for my part I want a little more female society."

"Female society is it you want?" replied Bridger; "why, man, there's some twenty thousand of it across the mountains, just one hundred and thirteen miles; and you'll be in the thick of it before June. Can't you wait till then?"

"But, Uncle Jim," returned the lieutenant, "I don't believe, from all I've heard about the folks in the valley, that it's the kind that I care for."

"You're a derned sight too proud for your business, young man," hotly responded Bridger. "I know that you're an eddicated cuss, but my natteral eye for a woman is as sharp as yours. For ten year and more, down yonder on the fork, I've seen every handcart train that forded Green River bound for the [Great Salt] lake, and you're out in your reck'ning if you think you can't find as eddicated women in the valley as any you've got at home. Now, there's Sam Peckham's wives,"[24] continued the old man, while he filled his pipe; "there was sixteen of 'em when I last heard of Peckham, and the last time I saw 'em myself was three year ago, when I was over in the city a-bargaining of the old fort to Lew Robinson [sic].[25] We went up to Peckham's to sign the papers, and there was

---

24 Samuel Whitney Richards had five wives in 1858 and ultimately had as many as ten.
25 Lewis Robison was born on October 28, 1816, in Cincinnati, Ohio and died on November 1, 1883, in Salt Lake City. In 1858 Robison (not "Robinson") was a brigadier general in the Nauvoo Legion and its quartermaster general. He was long Brigham Young's principal agent in the Fort Bridger/Green River area. Here Jim Bridger refers to his negotiations to sell his fort to Young before being driven out in 1853. Richards would not have been involved in those negotiations, but Browne has used this as a means of linking Jim Bridger to Jane Mayer, who did not arrive in Salt Lake until 1855.

Jane Moore,—his fourth. I tell you, young man, that you'll s'arch far and long in York city for such a woman as she is."

"Who's Sam Peckham?" struck in the quartermaster, joining our group by the fireside and stirring his mug with an iron spoon as he approached.[26]

"Who's Sam Peckham?" responded Bridger, repeating the question. "Why, Captain John, I'd 'a' suspected you'd 'a' known more 'n that about the people over in the valley that you're going to do your trading with next summer, if you can get within bargaining distance of 'em. Sam—why, he's clear 'way up nigh the top of the whole Mormon pack. Not a picter [picture] card but about a ten spot.[27] He's one of the twelve apostles. You see Sam had a way of keeping in with the right and left bowers and the other picter cards,—I mean Brigham and Heber [C. Kimball] and the rest of the saints high in glory,—and he made a good thing out of it, and he's got about as many flocks of all kinds, two-legged or four-legged, as any of the fellers in the Old Testament that they like to preach about in the Mormon Tabernacle. He was their Perpetooal 'Migration[28] Agent five year, more or less, shipping all the saints from England; and he kind of set his brand on the purtiest there was, and when they got as far along as the top of the bench above the city, the whole lot of picter cards was there and picked

26　The Utah Expedition's able quartermaster at Camp Scott was Capt. John H. Dickerson.

27　In Jim Bridger's playing-card analogy, Samuel W. Richards was a "ten," just below the value of the face cards he assigned to the apostles, who outranked Richards in the church's hierarchy. The "bowers" were probably the two counselors in Brigham Young's First Presidency.

28　The Perpetual Emigrating Fund, established in 1849, assisted poor members of the Church of Jesus Christ of Latter-day Saints, especially those from abroad and the eastern U.S., in traveling to Utah. Leonard J. Arrington, *Great Basin Kingdom: An Economic History of the Latter-day Saints, 1830–1900. New edition* (Urbana: University of Illinois Press, 2005).

'em out from the hand-carts accordin' to the marks that the 'postle to the Gentiles had writ over aforehand.[29] But Sam,—he was an old head! He'd got a kind of privit brand of his own, and he sent along only five marked with it, which all was saved up for him. But when he come back hisself he brought eleven more in a lump."

"Now, Jane Moore, as I was a-saying," continued the old man, addressing himself again to the young lieutenant, who sat drumming with his fingers on the bottom of the tin mug which he had emptied and turned upside down, "Jane was Sam's fourth, and was one of them that come ahead. I was there the day they crossed the fork. First there come some cows an twenty or thirty women a-wading across, and then there come a string of hand-carts, with pervisions and furniture and babies in 'em, and the men a-hauling and a-pushing of 'em, and then there come a wagon with two sisters and a piano and a looking-glass with a gold frame—as handsome a looking-glass as you'll find in any bar-room in St. Louis—and a sick woman in the bottom of the wagon along with the piano, and then there come Jane and Henerietta."[30]

"I suppose that Henerietta," interrupted the lieutenant, adopting Bridger's superfluous syllable, "was Sammy's fifth."

"You're wrong there, lieutenant," said Uncle Jim, "as you'd found

---

29   Writing to her mother in Great Britain about her arrival in the Salt Lake Valley with the Hunt wagon company in November 1856, one disgruntled pioneer woman who remained in Utah less than two years, wrote: "The Mormons made them [the arriving pioneer company] pay tithings of the clothes they had on their backs, and everything else they had, and they were obliged to get married to get something to eat and something to wear. . . . I was not a little surprised to see the men running after the women and asking them if they were married, but I have not got married yet, and I do not intend." Elizabeth Cotton, "A Picture of Life Amongst the Mormons," *The Cardiff and Merthyr* [*Tydfil, Wales*] *Guardian,* May 8, 1858, 7.

30   It is unlikely that the Polydore-Mayer party was traveling with a piano, but years earlier first counselor Heber C. Kimball had transported one across the plains. In the spring of 1858, he loaned it to Governor Cumming's wife, Elizabeth, for her use in the rented Staines Mansion in Salt Lake City.

out soon if you hadn't been so quick. Henerietta was the purtiest eight-year-old girl that ever I saw afoot with a hand-cart train; and Jane, she was over-young looking to be her mother.[31] Well, they two stood atop of the bank, up in the greasewood, watching the wagon slant down the cut in the clay to the fork. But when the steers touched water they just shied off sideways, and the [wagon] tongue it snapped short off, and the wagon slipped on the off-wheels and just tipped the whole load into the fork,—the piano and the sick woman and the looking-glass. The woman, she floated; and the looking-glass, it smashed; and we hooked the piano out chock full of water, and carried the whole of 'em up to the fort. It was hard to pull that looking-glass all the way from Ioway city and smash it just here almost in sight of the Promised Land."

Here Bridger paused for a moment, utterly absorbed in a silent calculation of the cost of the looking-glass and its transportation, and the total loss by the breakage, and I doubt whether he ever would have regained the thread of the story but for Captain John, who broke the pause by asking, "Whereabouts on the bank do you say that you left Jane and Henerietta standing four years ago, Uncle Jim? If they're still there, I'll send down to-morrow morning and fetch them up to camp. It's cold weather for an 'eddicated' woman and girl to be out so long."

"That ain't fair, Captain John," said Bridger. "As soon as we'd picked the sick old woman out of the fork, we took her up to the fort, and she died there two days after. I observed that she took to the Christian scripters, instead of Jo Smith's Mormon Bible, for her dyin' consolations.[32] She was a poor old creeter from Cornwall. Lots of 'em come from thereabouts. It's a mining country,

---

31 Jane E. Mayer had been born in 1831.
32 Here Browne has Bridger subscribing to the enduring perception outside the church that Latter-day Saints were not Christians. They strongly assert that they are Christians, but not Protestants.

as I've heerd, and I s'pose that the poor creeters who live in the burrows there think that everything that sunlight lays on must be as good as it is bright. If it wa'n't so, there wouldn't be so many of 'em trapped by such smooth-tongued fellers as Sam Peckham.[33] We buried the old woman just behind the northeast corner of the fort, inside of that place that your artillery major [captain] has put up with a brass [field] gun in it. He calls it a demi-lunette,[34] but it looks to me like any other ornery stone-wall. I took Henerietta on to my old shoulders, with her purty little ankles hanging one down on each side, and carried her across the water on my back."

Just here the adjutant entered the tent with my bundles of dispatches, sealed, and securely bound with red tape.[35] The last farewell was soon said, and I was wandering through the camp to warn my companions to be ready betimes in the morning.

Our party was in the saddle by star-light, before the first streak of dawn glimmered above the eastern bluff, and when Camp

---

33   Many such immigrants were hard-rock (tin) miners from England's Cornwall district. Throughout the American mining frontier, they were nicknamed "Cousin Jacks."

34   Embarrassed by the success of the Nauvoo Legion's raids on his supply trains on the trail, when Gen. Johnston reached the charred remains of Fort Bridger, he immediately set out to strengthen the post's defenses. This included building two artillery emplacements (lunettes) atop the surviving cobblestone walls and installing some of Captain Phelps's brass field pieces. For a contemporary sketch of these fortifications, see MacKinnon, ed., At Sword's Point, Part 1, 451.

35   Browne may have described the bundling of the dispatches this way because of his lingering embarrassment in 1877 over not realizing in January 1858 that some of the papers were intended for delivery along the way to Forts Laramie and Kearny as well as Leavenworth. This mistake was not discovered until he arrived at General Scott's headquarters in New York, the address on the outer wrapper. This delivery blunder caused a delay of several weeks in awareness at Laramie of how badly the Utah Expedition needed supplies from that post. For General Scott's explanation of this incident and judgment that "Mr. Brown[e] is not considered by the General-in-Chief accountable for this error," see Asst. Adjt. Gen. McDowell to Col. Samuel Cooper, March 1, 1858, "Report of the Sec. of War (1858)," 39.

Scott awoke to another day of its monotonous life, we were ten miles away on the trail to Henry's Fork,[36] where we were to select our horses and pack-mules from the herds which were pasturing there near the dragoons' camp. That evening a courier from Camp Scott brought down to me another package of dispatches, and a letter from the general's aide, the young lieutenant, which inclosed [sic] one of the neat little three-cornered notes in which the pass-words for the day were usually communicated to those who were entitled to them. Opening it, I read:—

HEADQUARTERS CAMP SCOTT,
January 8, 1858.
Parole: *Jackson and New Orleans.*[37]
Countersign: *Henerietta's ankles.*[38]

The next morning we were far away on our bleak journey to the States,—a journey of a thousand miles through snow-drifts, in which we should find only two spots where there was a roof that sheltered a white man.[39]

---

36 In late November 1857, because of the better availability of winter grass, Gen. Johnston sent the expedition's horses and mules to Henrys and Smiths forks of the Snake River, where they grazed under guard by the Second Dragoons, whose troops resented the isolated, unsoldierly duty after their agonizing march from Fort Laramie.

37 An allusion to Gen. Andrew Jackson's defeat of the British at New Orleans on January 8, 1815. For most of the nineteenth century this date was celebrated as an unofficial holiday in much of the United States. Either unwittingly or by design, Browne has skewed the chain of events and timing of his departure for the East by several days. He and his party left Camp Scott on January 5.

38 Browne's repeated references to ankles calls attention to the boundaries of Victorian proprieties and does so in the setting of a frontier army bivouac populated by men almost wholly without female companionship.

39 Probably Forts Laramie and Kearny, if not John Baptiste Richard's trading post at Platte Bridge or another one at Green River.

A. G. Browne's Scrapbook of His Published "Tribune" Dispatches, including a brief hand-written description of his 1858 winter trek between Fort Bridger and the Atlantic Coast. *Courtesy of Special Collections, J. Willard Marriott Library, University of Utah.*

"Weary and on the Verge of Sickness"

HARD GOING ON THE MORMON TRAIL

❧ EDITORIAL NOTES

This section, more than any of the other five, is a blend of fact, pure fiction, and a combination of the two. The several pages dealing with Browne's eastbound trek are largely accurate. Because of the need for secrecy in 1858, this material is virtually the only record of his winter trail experiences; his companions left none. However, in his 1859 Utah Expedition essay for The Atlantic Monthly, *Browne did publish a brief description of this mission that was unattributed and written in the third person:*

> The dispatches in which these [Johnston's] anxieties were commu-
> nicated to General Scott, together with suggestions for their relief,
> were intrusted in midwinter to a small party for conveyance to the
> States. The journey taught them what must have been the sufferings
> of the expedition which Captain [Randolph B.] Marcy led to Taos.
> Reduced at one time to buffalo tallow and coffee for sustenance, there
> was not a day during the transit across the mountains when any
> stronger barrier than the lives of a few half-starved mules interposed
> between them and death by famine. All along the route lay memorials
> of the [November 1857] march of the army, and especially of Colonel

[Philip St. George] Cooke's [dragoon] battalion,—a trail of skeletons
a thousand miles in length, gnawed bare by the wolves and bleaching
in the snow, visible at every undulation in the drifts.[1]

What Browne endured as Albert Sidney Johnston's courier he held private until 1877, revealing it only with the publication of Ward. In 1913 his Harvard classmates attributed his death in 1891 to "a disease dating probably from the privations encountered in the Utah Expedition, from which he had suffered for many years with fortitude."[2]

Jo Brooks' account of the 1855 suffering of a Mormon handcart company beset by "ship-fever" west of Fort Laramie and pusillanimous behavior by army officers is an inaccurate conflation of several events of which Browne had no first-hand knowledge: the 1849 cholera epidemic in the Mississippi River Valley and its spread along the Oregon Trail, and the 1856 Willie-Martin handcart disaster caused by a late start across the Great Plains, inadequate provisioning, and brutal weather. The use of head-boards from a Mormon burial site for firewood reflects Browne's use (and rearrangement) of one of his 1858 Tribune dispatches. This incident occurred not in February during Browne's January eastbound trek but rather in May as he traveled west with the Hockaday Mail to return to the Utah Expedition

---

1   [Browne], "The Utah Expedition: Its Causes and Consequences," 478. For a documentary account of the marches of Captain Marcy and Colonel Cooke, the longest and most arduous winter treks in American military history, see MacKinnon, ed., *At Sword's Point, Part 1*, 401–403, 467–68, and *Part 2*, 38–64. An additional way to understand Browne's winter trail experience is through Charles R. Morehead's reminiscences of his and wagon master Jim Rupe's passage over the same route ten days earlier. Theirs was a freezing, wolf-plagued ordeal that Morehead recalled with horror a half-century later. Morehead, "Morehead's Recollections" (Appendix C) in *War with Mexico, 1840–1847: Doniphan's Expedition and the Conquest of New Mexico and California*, by William E. Connelley (Topeka, Kans.: Crane & Company, 1907), 600–22.

2   Unattributed, "Albert Gallatin Browne," *Report of the Harvard Class of 1853*, 46–51. Browne's Boston death certificate indicated he suffered from diabetes.

after delivering his dispatches. Browne related the incident in a letter he sent to the Tribune on August 6, 1858, at which time he was safely in Salt Lake City. The account of Brooks' and the fictive "Bob Hutchins' " earlier engagement to guide two ladies and a young girl from St. Joseph, Missouri, to Salt Lake City was probably created from whatever Browne learned from Jane Mayer Richards during the summer of 1858 about her earlier travels. Meager as it is, this may be the most accurate account available of the westbound movement of Jane, Henrietta Mayer Polydore, and her daughter in 1855.

In describing his trip preparations before leaving Camp Scott, Browne omitted reference to the arrangement by which he entrusted the continued flow of unsigned dispatches to the Tribune to his young friend, David Auguste Burr, the New York Times' pseudonymous correspondent ("A.B.C."), who was also justice of the peace and coroner for Utah's Green River County and son of David H. Burr, Utah's controversial, non-Mormon surveyor general. That Burr would thus write simultaneously on the same subject for two competing Manhattan dailies without alerting his readers or editors was not then unusual, although it required ingenuity in phrasing and would be unethical today.[3]

It was near sunset on a bitter afternoon early in February, when we struck the Oregon trail. For two days we had not been able to collect fuel for a fire. The snow lay so deep on this part of the route across the dreary table-land that during the whole of the preceding week we were compelled to break the crust and trample a path ourselves, to make a passage

---

3   MacKinnon, ed., *At Sword's Point, Part 2*, 97.

for our animals, and we were fortunate to accomplish in this way
five or six miles between sunrise and sunset.[4] This day the ther-
mometer had marked eighteen degrees below zero at noon. Every
one of us was weary and on the verge of sickness, and several were
frost-bitten. But there was spirit enough left to raise a hearty
cheer when Jo Brooks, who led the trampling column and had
just surmounted a swell in the table-land, pointed to some dark
knolls in the distance and cried out, "The Sweetwater!"[5]

We toiled with renewed courage long after the yellow streaks of
sunset had faded into gray in the gloomy evening sky. The snow
became thinner after the crest of the bluff was turned which
bounded southward the bottom-lands of the stream, and soon
we were able to mount and press forward with increasing speed.
The outlines of the dark knolls grew more distinct in the dusk,
and were recognizable as the cliffs on the other side of the river.
At last we crossed the frozen ruts of the broad emigrant-road,
but did not rest until we reached the river-side at a bend where
the current was so swift that a strip a hundred feet long was free

---

4   Browne may not have experienced this ordeal, but may have been inspired by Cap-
     tain Marcy's accounts of his troops breaking trail for their mules on hands and knees
     as they crawled through the mountains in December 1857 on the way to Taos from
     Fort Bridger to purchase animals to remount and re-provision the Utah Expedition.
     See Marcy, "Expedition Across the Rocky Mountains," in *Thirty Years of Army Life
     on the Border* (New York: Harper & Brothers, 1866), 198–221. Browne would have
     first heard verbal accounts of Marcy's ordeal when the captain returned to Camp
     Scott in early June 1858 a few days after Browne's own return from the East.
5   The Sweetwater River is a long winding stream that passes through Devil's Gate and
     skirts Independence Rock along the overland trail before flowing into the North
     Platte River after a course of nearly 240 miles. "Jo Brooks" may have been the fictive
     name for Browne's guide, unless he meant W.J. Brooks, a seasoned mail conductor
     on this route. See "Later from Utah . . . The Weather in the Rocky Mountains," Dis-
     patch from "A.B.C." [David A. Burr], December 18, 1858, *New York Times*, January 26,
     1859, 2. As a practical matter, the real guide for Browne's party was not the "Brooks"
     character but John M. Hockaday, who had been over this route dozens of times with
     Hockaday-Magraw mail service between Independence and Salt Lake City.

of ice,—a welcome sight to our eyes, for ever since we began to ascend Bitter Creek, more than a fortnight [two weeks] before, we had obtained water only by melting the snow.

After unpacking the mules and turning them loose to pick a difficult meal of bunch-grass, the first care was to search for wild-sage bushes enough to make a fire for warmth and cooking. I remained by the pack-saddles while my companions dispersed on this business. The search was long, but one man after another brought his scanty tribute to the pile of brush, until the store was large enough to justify kindling part of it, and the first gleam of the blaze was greeted with shouts from the distant searchers.

Jo Brooks was the last to return to camp, and came loaded with an armful of boards, each three or four feet long and about a foot wide. My first thought was that he had happened upon a wagon which had been abandoned by the side of the trail; and I was just on the point of proposing that we should bring in the rest of the vehicle, when I recognized, by the light of the flame which sprang up as he cast one of the boards upon the smoking brush, the very different source from which he had obtained them. something in my look compelled Jo to an apology, which he was quick to make, and which took the tone of a defense.

"When I helped bury the poor creeturs, now three years ago, doctor," said he, "I never thought I'd have come to this. But somebody will suffer to-night, sir, after all the men have gone through these two days, unless this fire can be kept up till we get into marching order again, and I don't believe there's a single ghost among the whole of them as would grudge his wooden tombstone to keep a fellow from freezing. I never did the like of it but once before," Jo continued. "That was in the early spring of '52, ten miles the other side [east] of Fort Laramie. Two of us had gone out still-hunting [on foot] after buffalo, and were caught in a storm one afternoon, with the sleet driving right into our eyes so that we couldn't make a hundred yards an hour towards the fort; and we were soon out of our reckoning and quarreling about the points of the compass. It was near midnight when the storm held up, and it cleared off bitter cold. We were huddled in a gully, where we'd sought shelter below the top of the bluff, so that the body of the storm swept over our heads; but we were wet to the skin, and our clothes were frozen stiff to our backs. Bob Hutchins was the first to crawl out, and then came back almighty quick, looking scared. Just up above us, on the edge of the bluff, he had run square on to two of those kind of four-post bedsteads, sir, that the Sioux bury their dead on. Bob was thinking of ghosts, but the only thing I could get to thinking of was fire-wood. It took a while for me to pry Bob's courage up to the mark, but I got him up to it at last, and in less than half an hour we had both of those four-posters down, and everything there was on top of them, and we burned the whole of it that night. If we'd been seen or known by any of the Ogalallays[6] about the fort, the skin on our heads wouldn't have been worth insuring for ninety-nine and nine tenths per cent.; but two dead Injuns saved two live white men from freezing that night, and this 'ere lot of head-boards, sir, is going to help do the same by six more."

I brought the rest of the boards to the fire and examined them by the blaze. Some traces of red chalk were visible on one or two of them, but rain and snow in the three years had effaced all their meaning. Not a single word or figure was intelligible.[7] While I

---

6   The Oglala band of Sioux Native Americans.

7   In 1858 Browne described the head boards a bit differently: "I threw down my load, and then stooped to warm my hands at the fire which was just kindled, when I noticed on the board some words printed with red chalk, all of which that were distinguishable were 'Augusta, age 19.'" [Browne], "Later from Utah," Dispatch, August 6, 1858, New-York Tribune, September 6, 1858.

made the examination, Jo discoursed to his companions about the burying-ground which he had robbed of this lumber.

"I thought I knew the place, boys," said he, "the moment we turned the swell of the ground and caught sight of the river; but I wasn't dead certain of it, and if there's one thing more than another that I've learned in ten years' knocking round in these parts it is not to fire till I'm sure of my shot. It didn't seem to me, though, that there could be two bends in a hundred miles like this one; and so, while the rest of you were looking after the horses, I crossed the river on the ice, and, sure enough, there was the old ship-fever camp of 1855, where I was nurse. It was a Mormon hand-cart train. Somebody'd got ship-fever on the voyage, and it broke out bad among them before they got to Laramie. The major[8] wouldn't let them stop at the fort, but sent the army doctor[9] out to them with a lot of medicine; and somehow, after a while they crawled along as far as here, when they had to haul over across the river and set up a regular hospital for six weeks and more. Two thirds of the poor devils died and were buried yonder, and there isn't one of those boards that I didn't see as wet with tears as if it had been rained on."

At dawn, the next day, Jo and I started from the camp to gather up the mules, leaving the rest of the men busy arranging the packs and cooking the morning meal. When we were out of ear-shot I said to him, "You haven't kept good faith with me, Jo Brooks. You know as well as I do that I wouldn't have trusted you on this journey if I had suspected that you ever were a Mormon."

"I never was a Mormon, sir," answered Jo. "What makes you think I was?"

---

8   The post commander at Fort Laramie then was Maj. William Hoffman, Sixth U.S. Infantry.

9   Asst. Surg. Thomas Murray Getty.

"How did you happen to be traveling with a Mormon hand-cart train three years ago?" I replied.

"Bless your soul, sir," said Jo, "if that's what troubles you, I can make it clear enough in twenty words. You see I've been a good deal of a vagabond in my day, and in the spring of 1855 I was lying round loose in Saint Jo [St. Joseph, Missouri], ready for a job of any sort, and the job came along then in this fashion. There was a lady at the hotel, who had been there some days, waiting for another lady to come up the river. She came at last—this other lady—the whole way from New Orleans, alone except for a little girl there was with her. These two women were bound for Salt Lake, and Bob Hutchins was there to take them out,—the same fellow I told you of last night, sir. Bob was a sneaking kind of Mormon; that is to say, he was a hot one in the [Salt Lake] valley, and cooled off and made believe Gentile at the [Oregon Trail] forts or down in the States. He hired me to help, and we started out,—the two ladies, and Bob and I, and the little girl with us. The women and the girl rode in a four-mule wagon, with a piano and a big looking-glass, and tied themselves up of nights; and Bob and I, we drove on the front seat by day and slept outside by night on buffalo skins. We'd passed Laramie, say thirty miles, when we caught up with the sick hand-cart train; and the two women did what the major and the folks at the fort hadn't the stuff in them to do. They just went in among those poor devils as if they'd been their own flesh and blood; and what was more, they put Bob and me to nursing, too.[10] Bob was scared of the fever,—he always was a coward,—and the second night he cleared out and took the four mules along with him, and hide nor hair of that fellow has been

---

10   This incident was wholly fictive, with Browne doing a disservice to the troops of Fort Laramie in their efforts to help emigrants, including Latter-day Saints on the overland trail.

seen in these parts since. While we were lying here, a party of Mormons from the valley came along, going East, and the ladies paid me off, and one of them turned about and went back with the missionaries. But I stood by the camp till what was left of the handcart people got a-going again, and then I bargained with some Oregon emigrants, that were passing, for a yoke of steers to pull the wagon with the other lady and the girl. I saw them all off on the way to the valley, and then I doubled back to Fort Kearney [*sic*] and hired myself out to the sutler there for that winter."[11]

"Yes," said I, "I know all about that. The little girl's name was Henrietta, and the name of the woman that went on with her was Jane Moore, and the other woman's name was—what was her name, Jo?"

"It was an uncommon name,[12] sir," said Jo, looking almost as frightened as Bob Hutchins when they burned the Indian mummies. "How did you know about all this, sir?"

"I shan't tell you, Jo," said I; "but do you pledge me your word of honor that you never were a Mormon?"

"I do, sir," replied Jo.

---

11 Established in 1848, Fort Kearny [not "Kearney"] was named after army Gen. Stephen Watts Kearny, not to be confused with Fort Phil Kearney named after another officer.

12 A veiled reference to "Polydore," or "Perego" as the novella rendered it.

THE UTAH EXPEDITION'S MARCH
THROUGH SALT LAKE CITY, JUNE 26, 1858

This image, contrived fifteen years after the event, was the first and most enduring depiction of the army's march through a city deserted and ready for the
torch. *Engraving (1873) from T. B. H. Stenhouse's book* Rocky Mountain Saints,
public domain.

"We Had Found and Captured Henrietta"

LEGAL PROCEEDINGS IN SALT LAKE CITY

❦ EDITORIAL NOTES

Because Browne's main focus in Ward *was Henrietta Polydore's story, he here by-passes most of his own adventures during the period between his arrival on the Sweetwater River in February and his return to Camp Scott/Fort Bridger on May 27. In the process he omitted all reference to the rest of his overland trek via Forts Laramie, Kearny, and Leavenworth, river passage to St. Louis, rail travel to army headquarters in Manhattan and his home in Salem, and journey to several of the executive departments in Washington. After wrestling with doubts about whether he should remain in the East rather than return to Utah, he headed west via Hockaday's new overland mail service based in St. Joseph, Missouri. Understandably, Browne chose not to describe an embarrassing incident in which he lost an important dispatch from Chief Justice Eckels to Secretary of State Lewis Cass when his luggage was stolen en route to Washington. It was a major loss from which Browne recovered by reconstructing Eckels' letter from memory once he reached the State Department.[1]*

---

1   See Browne to Cass, March 15, 1858, MacKinnon, ed., *At Sword's Point, Part 2,* 103–106.

Browne's description of the terrain between Fort Bridger and Salt Lake City, his profile of the town itself, and his account of the legal proceedings brought there in U.S. district court to retrieve and repatriate Henrietta are highly accurate. Why Browne chose to substitute "Perego" for the Polydore family's surname and alter father Henry's given name to "Julian" is as unclear as the substitution of "Moore" for Mayer, especially since he used unchanged so many other names, like those of Jim Bridger and Albert Sidney Johnston. Browne's landlord in Salt Lake was not "Josiah Baxter" but was Edward Cuthbert.[2]

Oddly, Browne failed to mention that on the day proceedings in the Polydore case began in Judge Eckels' courtroom, the general election was held in Utah for territorial offices and those for Salt Lake County. Elder Samuel W. Richards and Hosea Stout, Jane Mayer Richards' defense attorney, appeared on the "regular" (Latter-day Saint) ballot for seats in the territorial legislature's house of representatives, while attorneys Browne and McCormick ran for the same office on the "opposition" (non-Mormon) ticket. Of the 1,050 votes cast that day in Salt Lake City, Browne, McCormick, and their running mates garnered only thirty-seven. This lopsided outcome was to be different when these four men met later that day for a different contest in Salt Lake City's U.S. district court.[3]

One of the other surprises in this section is Browne's minimal treatment of the Utah Expedition's triumphant march through Salt Lake City on June 26, one of the war's most dramatic moments. There were so many troops, camp followers, wagons, and animals involved that it

---

2   Browne may have either forgotten his landlord's name or chosen to use "Baxter" because Cuthbert had an inappropriately genteel ring to it for the roughhewn family he was describing. Based on the 1860 Utah Census for Salt Lake County, it appears that Edward Cuthbert from Ireland was indeed a blacksmith, as Browne reported to Capt. Phelps, but one who was younger than his "Brother Baxter" and not polygamous.

3   For the election, see Juanita Brooks, ed., *On the Mormon Frontier: The Diary of Hosea Stout, 1844–1861*, 2 vols. (Salt Lake City: University of Utah Press and Utah State Historical Society, 1964), 2:662 (August 2, 1858).

took the army eleven hours to pass through the city. Browne, of course, witnessed this spectacle. He had staked out a premier vantage point on a Salt Lake street corner from which to view this march-through—the longest such military procession since General Winfield Scott's entrance into Mexico City ten year earlier. He wrote about Johnston's march at length for the Tribune, *but strangely he barely mentioned it in* Ward.

SIX MONTHS LATER, A BRILLIANT EVENING IN JULY, I was sitting with Peter Dotson, the United States marshal, upon the veranda of my little adobe cottage in Salt Lake City. I went to church in New York on Easter,[4] and saw the pretty girls and new spring bonnets; returned to the camp in May, across green plains and torrents laughing in the sunshine, where so little while ago there stretched dreary wastes laced by icebound rivers; and entered the Mormon capital in June, a few days after the peace commissioners who carried President Buchanan's pardon to Brigham and Heber and the rest of Uncle Jim Bridger's "picter-cards" and "ten spots," Sam Peckham included.[5]

As we rode through Echo Canyon we inspected with curiosity

---

4   Based on his mother's diary, Browne was in Boston, not New York, on Easter Sunday, April 14, 1858.

5   Browne's delight in re-crossing the Plains on which he had nearly frozen to death during the previous winter was evident from the dispatch he sent to the *New-York Tribune* as he headed west toward Fort Bridger in mid-May: "Here I am . . . again upon the turf at the foot of the hill in Ash Hollow [Nebraska Territory]. Lying in this soft sunshine, I do not envy the most luxurious of the Turks the cushions of his divans or his chibouque and Latakia [exotic pipe and tobacco]. I challenge the whole Orient to rival the Occidental luxuries I enjoy in my pile of buffalo robes and pipe full of *kinnikinnik* [Indian tobacco]. In this Arcadia there is an independence of starched collars and tight boots which is delightful after a two-months sojourn among the conventionalisms of New-York and Boston." [Browne], "On the Way to Utah," Dispatch, May 14, 1858, *New-York Tribune*, June 12, 1858.

the rude embankments which the saints threw up against the approach of the army.[6] Then we crossed the Weber River,[7] traversed a chain of romantic gorges, climbed a steep pass of the Wasatch range, and at last began the descent into the valley of the Salt Lake. All along the slope of the mountain the path was lined with rose-bushes in full bloom, with clusters of columbines, and with party-colored tufts of wild flowers drooping under the weight of rain-drops. A dense mist sprinkled the hill-sides, so that we did not obtain our first view of the beautiful city until we emerged from Emigration Canyon.[8] Then the sky was clear overhead, and the sun was burning away the clouds from all the summits of the western mountains. But they still clung to the peaks which bound the valley on the southeast, and there they almost covered the snow on the crests of the range. At our feet lay the deserted Mormon capital, embowered in foliage. The line of the Great Salt Lake glittered on the western horizon.

The transition from the misty gloom of the mountain gorge was so sudden that the whole party uttered a cry of delight. We spurred our ponies over the slope, those of the company who had lived in the city pointing out the prominent buildings as we galloped along,—the tinned cupola of the City Hall, the Mansion

---

6   Echo Canyon, which originates near the southwestern corner of Wyoming and ends at the Weber River, was a long and important thoroughfare through the mountains east of Salt Lake City in Summit County. Used by Pony Express riders, pioneer wagon trains, and other travelers, fortifications were built on canyon hill-sides at several places during the Utah War to defend Utah, if necessary, from the approaching army.

7   The Weber River (pronounced "wee ber" not "webb er") rises in the Uinta Mountains south of Fort Bridger and flows northwest past the mouth of Echo Canyon and into the Great Salt Lake.

8   Emigration Canyon starts in the Wasatch Mountains east of Salt Lake City with its City Creek flowing through the heart of Salt Lake City into the Jordan River.

[Beehive] and Lion House of Brigham Young,[9] the structures in Temple Square, and the arsenal. Adown the valley, on each side of the great southern road, lay broad fields of grain to which the showers had imparted a lively green. Through the plain we could trace the windings of the Jordan by the glitter of the sunlight on its bends. As at last we clattered through the city, not a soul was visible except a group of half-naked Indian boys paddling in one of the rivulets which flowed along the gutters.[10]

The night of our arrival, Dotson, who was an old settler and

---

9   "City Hall" may have been a reference to the Council House in Salt Lake City—the first public building built in Utah. The Beehive House, named for a large wooden beehive that still sits atop the building, was one of Brigham Young's homes that also served as church headquarters for many years. Built next door to the Beehive House, the Lion House (named after a statue placed over the building's front door) was home for up to twelve of Brigham Young's wives and his children with them.

10   Since he had not been back to Utah in nearly twenty years, Browne's descriptions here of the terrain and flora between Fort Bridger and Salt Lake City, including the Nauvoo Legion's abandoned fortifications in Echo Canyon, relied heavily on the dispatch he sent to the *Tribune* dated June 17, 1858. To a certain extent, this and other reports, in turn, used phraseology borrowed liberally but without attribution from an earlier letter sent to Browne (still at Fort Bridger) from Salt Lake City by David A. Burr, who had traveled to the city independently and a week or so ahead of the army. Browne used Burr's descriptions with the latter's consent, and paid him for what was, in effect, advance knowledge of what Browne could expect to see once he himself started to travel the 113 miles between the Utah Expedition's soon-to-be-abandoned winter quarters and what some called the "City of the Saints." Using Burr's material, Browne was able to save the time and effort of composing lengthy descriptions himself and perhaps was able to "scoop" his journalistic competitors at Fort Bridger by providing *Tribune* readers with early information about a region that he and others had not yet seen since Brigham Young had sealed the territory's borders in September 1857. [Browne], "Important from Utah," Dispatch, June 17, 1858, *New-York Tribune*, July 19, 1858; David A. Burr, Letter to Albert G. Browne and James W. Simonton, June 9, 1858, Burr Family Papers (Collection #1333), Special Collections, Krock Library, Cornell University, Ithaca, N.Y. A typescript of this letter is among the holdings in Mortimer Rare Book Room, Neilson Library, Smith College, Northampton, Mass., and it is available in published form in MacKinnon, ed., *At Sword's Point, Part 2*, 513–20.

had been "run off" by the Mormons in 1856, took quiet possession of his house, which consisted of one bedroom, a kitchen, and a pantry, and gave accommodation there and in the yard to the civil officers of the territory, for three or four weeks, until the Mormons returned to the deserted city and Brigham gave permission to the saints to let us lodgings.[11] During this time I inhabited a huge covered wagon, one of the well-known "arks of the plains," which I wheeled into the yard. I used to climb into it at night on a short ladder, which I pulled up after me; and truly there were such attractions in that mediaeval style of life that I quitted the old ark with a good deal of regret, to take quarters just across the broad street, in Elder Josiah Baxter's one-story adobe, of which I secured a lease at an exorbitant rent for six months.[12]

---

11   Peter K. Dotson, a non-Mormon, emigrated to Utah from what is now West Virginia in 1850. Initially he partnered with Brigham Young in the operation of a brewery and then became entangled in the local religious-political conflicts while in partnership with John M. Hockaday in a Salt Lake City tannery. In 1856 President Pierce appointed Dotson U.S. marshal for Utah when the incumbent, a Latter-day Saint, was removed for brawling in the offices of the treasury department in Washington while trying to settle his accounts with the U.S. government. After months of obfuscation in Utah and ineptness in Washington, Dotson assumed office at Camp Scott at the end of 1857 under the army's protection. His relationship with the Latter-day Saints was mixed. Although he was largely viewed locally as "anti," he was not one of the four federal appointees whom Brigham Young and dozens of prominent Utah leaders petitioned President Buchanan to remove literally as the U.S. Army marched through Salt Lake City. As discussed below, Dotson resigned out of frustration in the summer of 1859 and moved to what became Colorado Territory. In subsequent sections of *Ward*, Browne often refers to him as "The Marshal," rather than by name.

12   Browne may have camped for a while in a covered wagon, but he also described sleeping with other non-Mormon visitors rolled up in Mackinaw blankets on the back porch of the Brigham Young–owned Globe Restaurant. Ultimately, he rented a small adobe house he described to an army officer at Camp Floyd: "I have at last a *ranche*, in partnership with Mr. [David A.] Burr. Bro. Brigham has allowed Bro. Cuthbert, a simple-hearted (perhaps -headed) blacksmith, to rent his own property. We have a *salon* about 12 feet by 16; a bed-room about 7 feet by 11 [16?]; and a wash-room (or, if I wish to dignify it, a *dressing-room*.) about 4½ feet by 7. We have

The respect which the army showed for all the possible rights of property of the Mormons was one of the most remarkable instances of good discipline I ever have witnessed. A fortnight elapsed after our arrival before it reached the city. Meanwhile a few hundred Mormons—all men—had come up from their great camp on the western [eastern] shore of Lake Utah, where the population, withdrawn from their settlements, to the number of nearly thirty-five thousand souls, had overflowed the little town of Provo, and been squalidly lodged ever since the early spring in board shanties, wigwams, log-huts, bowers of willow branches covered with wagon-sheets, and even in holes dug into the hill-sides.[13]

The day the troops marched across the town these few hundred men forsook all the public places and watched sullenly, through chinks in barricaded windows, the passage of the blue columns which poured along the lonely streets from morn till sunset. Yet under such circumstances of opportunity and provocation not a single instance of trespass upon a house or a garden-plot could be

---

also a piazza about 3 feet wide. In the other half of the house lives a bow-legged Vulcan [blacksmith], Cuthbert's partner.

"Our furniture consists of a book-case well filled with 'law'—the property of Mr. [John M.] Hockaday—a secretary, half-a-dozen chairs, a table, a carpet, four spittoons, and two lounges—the property of the U.S.—and four tumblers, one candle-stick, one tin-pan (used for a wash-basin.) one bucket, several trunks, and a demijohn, all the property of ourselves.

"Mr. [1st Lt. Grier] Tallmadge promises me a speedy visit. I can desire nothing more pleasant than that you shall accompany him. I will try to show you all the lions, particularly the one over Brigham's porch." Browne to Capt. John W. Phelps, July 27, 1858, Stanley Snow Ivins Papers (MSS B31), Box 9, Fd 11, typescript, Utah State Historical Society. Tallmadge was Phelps' executive officer in Battery B of the Fourth U.S. Infantry. These quarters may have been where Judge Eckels conducted the Polydore hearing a week after Browne wrote Phelps.

13   The board shanties in Provo were cabins for Brigham Young's family and were fabricated from lumber hauled south from the Salt Lake Valley. The far cruder and makeshift accommodations devised by other refugees signaled the inequality of sacrifice evident in the Move South. See MacKinnon, ed., At Sword's Point, Part 2, 338–39.

PETER K. DOTSON (1823–1898),
UTAH'S U.S. MARSHAL
He became Henrietta's court-appointed
lead guardian in 1858 until her September
departure for the Atlantic Coast with Judge
Eckels' entourage. Older than either Browne or
McCormick and with southern manners and an
English wife, "Uncle Pete" was apparently able
to establish a rapport with young Henrietta as
others did not. *Post-Utah photo courtesy City-
County District Library, Pueblo, Colorado.*

recorded against a soldier, or even against any one of the thousands of teamsters or camp followers. The army pitched its tents
that night on the banks of the Jordan, below [and west of] the
city, and a few days afterwards moved quietly southward to a
permanent camp more than thirty miles away, leaving the twenty-one Gentiles who were crowded into Pete Dotson's little house
and yard alone among the Mormon inhabitants, who immediately began to return to the city by thousands. Their trains usually came up the valley from Provo by daylight, and were driven
into town after sunset; and from the airy lodgings which I occupied in Dotson's yard, I could hear, night after night, from dusk
to dawn, the incessant tapping of hammers as the boards with
which almost every door and window had been covered were torn
away. Elder Josiah Baxter, Dotson's neighbor, arrived among the
earliest, and I at once engaged the [right of first] "refusal" of his
cottage, which was conditioned upon his obtaining the consent
of Brigham to let it to a sinner like myself. We conducted the
negotiations in his cellar under circumstances of extreme damp-
ness and secrecy, and Brigham ratified the bargain, probably after

EDWARD CUTHBERT'S SALT LAKE CITY blacksmith shop
Cuthbert, an Irish convert, was Browne's landlord and the model for his fictive
"Elder Baxter." *Photo (1858) by David A. Burr. Used by permission, Utah State
Historical Society.*

devout consideration of the fact that the rate of rent amounted to
a bare-faced spoliation of the Gentile tenant.

On this balmy summer evening, then, Pete Dotson and I were
sitting upon the veranda, smoking our pipes. Elder Baxter and
the two aged Mrs. Baxters were hoeing in the garden (which he
had reserved to himself in the lease), and crooning the melodies
of their faith while they toiled in the moonlight. The elder was
of a morose turn of mind, and yet so practical withal that he
was well aware of the relation of rhythm to manual labor. I had
observed his method with the Mrs. Baxters before this evening.
They would start work to slow metre. His favorite hymn, to begin

with, I remember opened with a stanza alluding rather pointedly
to our invasion of the Territory, which ran,—

> The trials of the present day
> Require the saints to watch and pray,
> That they may keep the narrow way
>   To the celestial glory.[14]

The elder "deaconed"[15] off the first three verses, and both of
the Mrs. Baxters united with him in the fourth. They would hoe
down, say, two rows to this dismal tune, and then the elder would
strike up something a little more lively:

> A church without a prophet is not the church for me:
> It has no head to lead it; in it I would not be.
> But I've a church not made by man,
> Cut in the hills by Brigham's hand:
> A church with gifts and blessings;
> Oh, that' the church for me![16]

---

14   As Browne correctly remembered, this is the first stanza of the hymn "The Trials
     of the Present Day." Authored by Eliza R. Snow and originally titled "Celestial
     Glory," it appeared in Latter-day Saint hymnbooks until the middle of the twenti-
     eth century. Published in November 1843, it had no connection to the Utah War.

15   Presumably, Browne meant that Mr. Baxter sang or recited as a deacon would read
     during a church service.

16   This is an altered version of the closing lines of an untitled folksong published in the
     Nauvoo [Illinois] *Times and Seasons* newspaper on February 4, 1845. Those lyrics
     were:
>   A church without a Prophet is not the church for me;
>   A church without a gathering is not the church for me;
>   It has no head to lead it, in it I would not be;—
>   The Savior would not own it, wherever it might be.
>   But I've a church not built by men,
>   But I've a church that's called out,
>   Cut from the mountain without hands;
>   From false traditions, fears and doubts,
>   A church with gifts and blessings—
>   O, that's A gathering dispensation—
>   O, that's the church the church for me, &c. for me, &c.

and both Mrs. Baxters would thereupon fervently repeat,—

Oh, that's the church for *me!*

The elder's climax was reached in a sacred ditty entitled The Bridegroom's Supper:—

There's a feast of fat things for the righteous preparing,[17]
That the good of this world all the saints may be sharing;
For the harvest is ripe, and the reapers have learned
To gather the wheat that the tares may be burned.
Chorus. Come to the supper, come to the supper,
Come to the supper of the great bridegroom.[18]

I think they always had themselves in mind as the wheat, and their Gentile tenant as the tares. During this chorus both Mrs. Baxters would hoe spasmodically, while the elder would drop his hoe and accompany his voice with a violent clapping of his hands.

On the present occasion we had surmounted the trials of the present day, but had not yet been invited to the bridegroom's supper, when our attention was diverted from the singing by the arrival of two riders who galloped up to the veranda, hitched their horses carelessly, and in a minute or two were seated like us with their feet over the railing, to the certain disgust of the elder and his brides, for one of them wore a military uniform which the saints detested as the livery [attire] of their oppressors. It was the general's young aide, the compiler of the New Year's pastry at Camp Scott, and the author of the countersign of the 8th of

---

17 This is a paraphrase of Isaiah 25:6.
18 This is the opening stanza of "Hymn 35," authored by W. W. Phelps, included in the initial Latter-day Saint hymnbook in 1835 and in subsequent hymnals until the middle of the twentieth century. It appeared as recently as 1998 in the *Saints Hymnal* published by the Church of Jesus Christ (Bickertonites), headquartered at Monongahela, Pennsylvania.

January. His companion was the United States attorney for the Territory.[19]

"Look here, doctor," exclaimed the latter, after the first greetings were exchanged, "the general has shirked a pretty piece of work off on me, and I want you to help me through with it. These military folks (begging your pardon, lieutenant) beat civilians all hollow in shirking. If they can find somebody to indorse a paper over to, and to give them a receipt for it, that's all they ever care for;" and saying this he tossed into my lap a bundle of dispatches which the aide had brought from the camp.

"What is it all about?" I asked.

"Take them inside, and strike a light and read them," he replied; "then give me your answer to-night, for I must send word back what we can do about it, and as the lieutenant goes back tomorrow I should like to send by him."

So I left the three on the veranda cracking jokes upon old Baxter and his wives, whose voices were uplifted just then in the averment, "Oh, that's the church for me!" and, lighting a candle inside of the cottage, I read a series of documents which told the following story:—

Mr. Julian Perego was a gentleman of Spanish descent, who resided at St. Albans, in Hertfordshire, England, and possessed a comfortable fortune. Both he and his wife were Romanists, and in 1852 they put their child, a girl then six years old, at a Roman Catholic school in Norfolk. During the next year domestic difficulties arose between the husband and the wife, and in 1854 Mrs. Perego kidnaped the girl from the school and escaped with her

---

19   This was Washington Jay McCormick ("The Attorney"), a young Hoosier protégé of Judge Eckels. He held this appointment on an interim basis. The incumbent, Hockaday, had gone east in January with Browne in a successful effort to exchange this role for that of the mail contractor on the St. Joseph, Missouri–Salt Lake City route.

to North America. She was met in one of the Western States by her sister, who had emigrated from England a year or two before. The father received information that the mother and child came first to New Orleans and took passage up the Mississippi. Then he obtained tidings of the meeting with the sister; and then all traces of them were lost.[20] Mr. Perego possessed sufficient influence in 1855 to procure special instructions from the home government to the British consuls at New Orleans and some other American ports to assist him to regain his child, but when these instructions reached Louisiana Mrs. Perego and her daughter had departed up the river, and all his attempts to pursue them proved fruitless.

At last, early in March, 1858, he received a letter, dated at New Orleans, from John Hyde, a well-known Mormon refugee [apostate], which informed him that Mrs. Perego was again in that city, and that the child was living in Utah, under the assumed name of "Lucy," with her aunt, Jane Moore, who was a wife of Elder Samuel W. Peckham, an important Mormon dignitary.[21]

---

20 The preceding portion of this paragraph was either disguised or simply inaccurate, including the characterization of Henry F. Polydore's financial circumstances, which were precarious. In the underlying dispatch of August 5, 1858, Browne presented names and locations accurately.

21 John Hyde, Jr. was a young Mormon apostate whom the church had excommunicated in 1856 after he unexpectedly turned on it while beginning a troubled mission to the Hawaiian Islands. Hyde retaliated in 1857 by publishing a tell-all book titled *Mormonism: Its Leaders and Designs*. It was a volume just in time to provide westbound officers of the Utah Expedition with a sensational account of the society Hyde believed awaited them in Salt Lake City. Hyde followed up the book's appearance with a series of Atlantic Coast lectures and letters to newspaper editors dispensing draconian advice on how the Buchanan administration should prosecute the Utah War. By late 1857 Hyde had gravitated to New Orleans. There, immersed in the flow of emigrating Mormons, he learned the details of the earlier passage through town of Mrs. Polydore, Lalla, and Jane Mayer.

By early 1858 Hyde was at work on a Mormon-oriented novel he titled *Infatuation: A Fiction Founded on Fact*. It was a book loaded with sensational accounts of the supposed marital practices of elderly Mormon leaders among Utah's *(continued)*

The following extracts from the correspondence complete the narrative:—[22]

MR. JULIAN PEREGO *to the* EARL OF MALMESBURY, *the British Minister of Foreign Affairs, March 26, 1858.*

... "I have not seen either my wife or child since the abduction of the latter in 1854, and I have never been able to hold communication in any manner with my child. Now I am, as your lordship may well believe, most desirous alike to rescue my little girl, now twelve years of age, from the most improper hands to which she has been committed, and from the Mormons' society altogether, and to prevent Mrs. Perego from regaining possession of her; and it is to request from your lordship any aid which as minister for foreign affairs you may be able to afford me that I venture to intrude myself upon your notice. The mode (if any) in which you can best promote my object of saving my child from apparently almost inevitable ruin will doubtless suggest itself to

---

young women together with tales of female flight and pursuit that resonates with the Polydore saga and those that appeared later. Whether John Hyde knew Henry Polydore is unknown, but the role of Hyde's father as leader of the church branch in Cheltenham made mutual awareness a distinct possibility. Either because of such a connection or an unrelated grudge that Hyde Junior bore Samuel W. Richards, in March 1858 he chose to pass information about Henrietta's whereabouts in Utah to her father. Hyde's revelation reinvigorated Henry Polydore's hunt for the fugitives, focused it on Salt Lake City, and ignited what today would be called a nasty international child custody suit.

22 The excerpts from the following diplomatic, military, and administrative correspondence presented here by Browne were accurate with the exception of substitutions for certain names and places. Since he was intimately familiar with the case as one of Henry Polydore's attorneys in Salt Lake City, Browne had an insider's access to all of the relevant documents, most of which he published for the first time in his dispatch to the *Tribune* of August 5, 1858, and, of course, re-published in *Ward* during 1877. This is a vivid example of the value of Browne's writing—fiction as well as non-fiction—as a unique primary source of information about the Utah War. The complete, unexpurgated documents are in the U.K. National Archives at Kew and the U.S. National Archives in Washington, with photocopies in the research files of the editors.

your lordship; but premising that I yesterday addressed a letter to his excellency, Mr. [George M.] Dallas, the American minister in London, applying for any aid which he in his official capacity can afford me, I would most respectfully suggest that by your lordship's communication with the government of the United States on my case, and recommending it to their attention, they might be induced to issue orders to the commander of their forces now proceeding to the Mormon settlement, to the effect that on the capture of the Salt Lake City my daughter shall be committed to safe hands till I shall be apprised of the fact and I can go or send for her, or otherwise to aid me in recovering my daughter. The only apology I can offer to your lordship for thus intruding a matter so wholly domestic upon your attention is this: that, so far as I know, there is no course that I individually can pursue which it is at all probable would be attended with success.

BARON NAPIER, *British Minister at Washington, to* LEWIS CASS, *Secretary of State of the United States. May 24, 1858.*

"I have the honor to transmit to you herewith a copy of a letter addressed by Mr. Julian Perego, of St. Albans, Herts, England, to the Earl of Malmesbury, conveying an account of the circumstances under which his only daughter, Henrietta Perego, was abducted when eight years of age from his control and transferred to the Mormon settlement at Salt Lake City. Her majesty's government have instructed me to request that you will lend your good offices towards the recovery of the child by directing the military and civil authorities of the United States to afford such assistance as may be in their power to Mr. Perego, or his attorney, or to any of her majesty's consuls, with the view of securing the personal safety of the daughter and her restoration to her father."[23]

---

23 One of the major factors fueling the intensity of Henry Polydore's quest was his fear that his daughter might soon he forced into marriage prematurely *(continued)*

FRANCIS, 10TH LORD NAPIER
(1819–1898), BRITISH MINISTER
TO WASHINGTON
Middleman in the trans-Atlantic diplomatic
effort to retrieve Henrietta for her father,
Lord Napier relayed the wishes of the British
foreign office to the U.S. State Department,
and then, upon her arrival in Washington
during December 1858, forwarded her to
Liverpool under escort by a Royal Messenger.
Photo (1855) courtesy Library of Congress.

LEWIS CASS, *Secretary of State, to* JOHN B. FLOYD, *Secretary of War. May 26, 1858.*

"I transmit herewith the copy of a communication addressed to this department by Lord Napier, and have the honor to request that you will be so good as to cause the necessary inquiries to be set on foot by the military authorities of the United States, with a view to the restoration of the daughter to her father, in

---

and perhaps even polygamously under circumstances beyond his control and even knowledge. Mr. Polydore's interactions with John Hyde Jr. and sensational British press coverage of the Utah War would have stoked this anxiety. Had he known about it, which he did not, Polydore would have derived no comfort from the case of Mary Ann Williams, a Utah girl whose guardian complained in August 1858 that, without his knowledge, Apostle George A. Smith had sealed his ward in marriage as the sixteenth wife of John D. Lee, Brigham Young's religiously adopted son, when she was quite young. R. Wilson Glenn to Smith, August 19, 1858, George A. Smith Papers, Church History Library. There is confusion regarding how old Williams was at the time of her marriage. Glenn's letter declares she was born September 10, 1844, making her about thirteen years old. Federal census records record her estimated birth year as 1842 (1860 census), 1846 (1870 census), and 1844 (1880 census).

GEN. LEWIS CASS (1782–1866),
U.S. SECRETARY OF STATE AND SENIOR
MEMBER OF BUCHANAN'S CABINET
DURING THE UTAH WAR
Cass was Judge Eckels' organizational superior
and conveyed the British request for an
American intervention in the Polydore affair to
secretary of war Floyd before he handed-off to
Gen. Johnston and U.S. attorney McCormick
in Utah. *Photo (between 1855 and 1865) courtesy
Library of Congress.*

accordance with the wishes expressed by the British government on the subject."

COLONEL SAMUEL COOPER, *Adjutant-General of the United States Army, to the Commanding Officer of the Army in Utah, via Leavenworth City, Kansas. June 15, 1858.*

"The secretary of war desires that you cause inquiries to be instituted for the purpose of gaining information respecting the young woman alluded to in the inclosed [sic] letters, and should it appear that she is still among the Mormons that you adopt such measures as may seem to you advisable to bring about her release from their community and her restoration to her friends."

BREVET BRIGADIER-GENERAL ALBERT S. JOHN-STON, *commanding the Department of Utah, to the United States Attorney for the Territory, July 27, 1858.*

"I presume that the duties enjoined upon me in my military capacity in the inclosed correspondence were expected to be performed in the contingency that the relations of the people of this

Territory to the federal government should be still unchanged on the reception of the instructions. Now, inasmuch as there has been an amicable adjustment of the difficulties heretofore existing, and the supremacy of the law is reestablished, I do not doubt that under the circumstances the design of the department will be fully accomplished by my handing over the papers to the civil authority, that such proceedings may be instituted as shall lead to the recovery of the little girl and her restoration to her father, in accordance with the request of the British minister, who asks the interposition of our government for that purpose."

I instantly recognized, of course with some astonishment, that the subjects of these dispatches were the heroines of Bridger's discourse the night before I left the winter camp on Black's Fork, and of Jo Brooks' story on the bank of the Sweetwater, both of which had frequently come back to my mind during the intervening months. Folding up the papers and leaning out of the window, I heard the group on the veranda discussing the chances of discovering the little Henrietta. Baxter and his wives had ceased crooning and hoeing, and had gone to bed.

The attorney was relating how, soon after the receipt of the dispatches, a few hours ago, he had sent a trusty person to Sam Peckham's house to ask if the fourth Mrs. Peckham had come up yet from Provo.[24] The messenger was received by the first Mrs. Peckham,[25] a sage woman, who suspected at once some secret purpose in the inquiry, and asked for a clearer specification of the wife in question, to which the messenger had replied that

24 The subtle but important implication here is that Jane and "Lalla" had been participating in the Move South, for which Provo was the major marshalling place pending determination of an ultimate haven at a more distant location commonly believed to be Mexican Sonora.
25 Mary Haskin Parker Richards, whom Samuel had married in 1846.

her name was Jane Moore, whereupon Sister Peckham denied stoutly that she had now, or ever had, any conjoint wife of that name.[26] Dotson, after cursing the imprudence of the messenger, was declaring his purpose to find the girl and her aunt though he should search for them a year; but one of the others availed himself of the well-worn illustration of the needle and the hay-stack.

I caused not a little wonder, therefore, when I said hopefully to the attorney, "I'll take the case with you, and if Peter will give me the appointment of a deputy-marshal I'll engage to find the girl within a week."

"I won't appoint a Mormon," said Dotson.

"It isn't a Mormon that I want," I replied; "it's a fellow named Jo Brooks, who was one of the men that went to the States with me last winter. I hear he came back this summer with a wagon train; and the chances are ten to one that the lieutenant can lay hand upon him over in the camp within twenty-four hours. If I can't have him, I want Uncle Jim Bridger; and if I can't have Uncle Jim—well, I might be willing to put up with the lieutenant there, if he'll take off his [officer] shoulder-straps and enter the civil service."

"What in thunder do you mean?" exclaimed the person last described.

"Don't you remember," said I, "the bogus countersign you sent me down on Henry's Fork last January? Just remember that, and think of names, and you'll begin to get some light about this girl and her aunt."

"By Jove, they are the very pair that old Bridger was talking about," broke out the lieutenant, evidently recalling the evening in the general's tent.

---

26   In court papers Jane also denied that she was married to Richards, which Browne would have known.

Then in a few words I told them about Brooks and the burying-ground on the Sweetwater.

The Lieutenant rode back to camp the next day with a let-ter assuring the general that the attorney, with my assistance, would undertake the case, and requesting a modest remittance of money for the expenses of the search. In reply, Jo Brooks was sent over to report to me; but we were advised that according to the ordinary course of affairs at Washington no provision had been made of any fund for executing the business enjoined in the dispatches; that probably Mr. Cass, Mr. Floyd, and Lord Napier, and the other distinguished gentlemen enumerated in the letters, "counted upon the benevolence of the legal profession." Lawyers, like physicians, were expected to practice free for ministers' fam-ilies, and here were concerned no less than two ministers for for-eign affairs and one at war, besides one envoy extraordinary and minister plenipotentiary.

"I suppose," remarked the attorney dryly, as we finished the reading of the general's unsatisfactory epistle, "that we might throw in Sam Peckham for the fifth minister concerned, consid-ering that he's one of the twelve apostles."

We were too deep in the case, however, by this time, to retreat for any pecuniary cause; and so that very afternoon Brooks was sworn in as a deputy marshal, intrusted with a writ of *habeas cor-pus* which we had sued out in the father's name, and put on the search for the child.[27] Not to make a long story of his adventures, his previous acquaintance enabled him to discover her and her

---

27   Jo Brooks' role as described here was fictive; the writ was served by Marshal Dot-son. One of the more intriguing mysteries is who devised the legal gambit of seeking a writ of *habeas corpus* ("produce the body") to retrieve Henrietta. There is no sign that Henry Polydore, a British solicitor, was involved. The likelihood is that the chief strategist was Browne, who was better educated and more experienced than McCormick.

aunt within a few days, and the writ was served and return was promptly made to it in the aunt's name by Brigham Young's former attorney-general, Hosea Stout, a hot-headed old polygamist, who indiscreetly admitted in the return almost all the facts which we desired to prove.[28]

The hearing before the judges[29] was held in Elder Baxter's cottage, for it contained the largest room of which any of the Gentiles in the city at that time had possession, since Brigham, while granting his followers leave to let us lodgings, had not yet conceded a place for the business of the courts. My board bedstead, turned up on edge and covered with buffalo robes, was the judicial bench; the judges and the counsel were accommodated with seats on barrels and soap-boxes; and Jane and Henrietta occupied my only two chairs. The chief-justice told me long afterwards, in confidence, that the top of the barrel, covered with a striped Navajo blanket, on which he sat gave way at a critical stage of the proceedings, but that a keen sense of the dignity of his office rescued him from the ordinary consequences of such a mishap, and enabled him to sit out the rest of them on the sharp edge of the staves.

The day before the hearing the general sent us private word that he would order a squadron or two of cavalry over to the city, if we apprehended a violent interruption of the trial; but after a

---

28   The legal papers are in Utah State Archives, Salt Lake City. Stout was also a brigadier general and the Nauvoo Legion's judge advocate general. His role in the Polydore case may be traced through his diary and the most recent biography, Stephen L. Prince, *Hosea Stout: Lawman, Legislator, Mormon Defender* (Logan: Utah State University Press, 2016).

29   For this case, Judge Eckels was joined on the bench by another federal jurist, who had just arrived in town, Charles E. Sinclair of Virginia. Sinclair had just turned thirty and was ridiculed by Brigham Young as "the boy" or "the cub." He soon acquired a local reputation as a spectacular drunkard.

consultation between the marshal and the judges the offer was declined, although, to tell the truth, every one of us was sensible that there would be serious risk of an outbreak.[30] The hour fixed for the hearing was three o'clock in the afternoon [of August 5], and the marshal took the prudent precaution to pack the room beforehand with all the Gentiles there were in the city. Admittance, however, was given to as many Mormons, and a crowd of one or two hundred saints occupied the yard below the veranda, and gazed curiously in through the open windows. I doubt whether there was a man in the room (the judges included) who did not carry a "six-shooter" in his pocket or under his coat tail, and a single shot would have been the signal for a "free fight." But the trial was conducted quietly, and even solemnly. The testimony of Jo Brooks, combined with the incautious admissions of the return to the writ, made a perfect case; judgment was awarded for the discharge of Henrietta from the custody of the aunt and her delivery to us as the representatives of the father, and at sunset on the 4th [5th] of August the marshal, the attorney, and myself were left alone with the child in our possession.[31]

Sam Peckham did not appear in person. The aunt was a neatly dressed woman twenty-eight or thirty years old, reserved in her manner, and bearing a manifest impress of education and polite associations. Remembering Bridger's description of her, I credited the old guide with accidentally telling the truth. Her self-possession and that of the child were perfect. Evidently they had been instructed beforehand as to the probable result, and had concerted their demeanor. So, when the judgment was pronounced,

---

30   Gen. Johnston made no such proffer of troops and the case generated little interest in Salt Lake, including on the part of Brigham Young.

31   Judge Eckels' decision actually made marshal Dotson Henrietta's sole custodian or "guardian."

she quietly delivered the child to the marshal, took Hosea Stout's arm, and swept out of the room with the air of a grand lady. The child did not shed a tear or make an exclamation, and sat bolt upright in her chair while the audience dispersed, nor did she offer to stir when the senior Mrs. Baxter entered the room and began to remove the barrels and soap-boxes, brush the floor, and put the scanty furniture to rights.

The conversation while the old woman was at work was reserved, for she clearly was bent on playing eavesdropper. At last, having garnished the house, and no pretext offering for a longer stay, the elder's wife could contain herself no longer. Perching her left elbow on the handle of her broom for a rest, and shaking her right hand defiantly at the marshal, who had not scrupled to intimate that we wished to be left to ourselves, she addressed us as follows:—

"Ain't you ashamed of yourselves, you despoilers of the helpless and violators of the innocent, to be sittin' here in council over this 'ere ewe lamb? Dog on [doggone] you, Peter Dotson," she proceeded, directing her indignation specially at the marshal, "if I'd 'a' known what you were a-plottin' this last week, I'd 'a' saved that young thing's soul, and sealed [married] her to a saint in glory, if I had had to make my Josiah take her his own self."

With this the young girl arose from her chair, and walking quickly to the window where I was standing, and from which I turned as she advanced, struck me a sudden and vigorous blow with her clinched fist in my face.[32]

"Glory hallelujah!" exclaimed Sister Baxter, escaping rapidly through the door-way, "the child's got the Holy Spirit in her, and all the powers of hell can't snake it out."

---

32   There is no evidence that this incident happened. It was devised for dramatic effect and as a precursor to Henrietta's parting message before boarding the *Africa* in New York harbor the next December (Section V).

A few minutes afterward we heard the old woman hoeing in her garden-plot and singing dolefully in her usual strain:—

> The trials of the present day
> Require the saints to watch and pray,
> That they may keep the narrow way
>   To the celestial glory.

We had found and captured Henrietta. What to do with the little vixen now was the serious question.

SECTION IV.

"What to Do with this Extraordinary Child"

GUARDIANS THREE

✣ EDITORIAL NOTES

When Albert Browne wrote about Henrietta in 1858 for the Tribune, *he said a great deal about her circumstances but almost nothing about her as a person, noting only: "She is an intelligent and interesting girl of now twelve years of age and whatever may have been the influence exerted over her during the last four years, it is especially fortunate that she has been rescued at this time. Had another year passed without the successful intervention of the father, she would probably have been betrothed, if not married, to a polygamist." It fell to other correspondents to describe her more fully, as with a reporter of the* St. Louis Democrat *who represented Henrietta as "a young English lady. . . a fine specimen of English beauty" and "a rosy-cheeked, fair-haired child."[1] In this fourth section of* Ward *written twenty years later, Browne takes artistic license to transform Henrietta's appearance and demeanor dramatically. Similarly, in 1877 Browne described*

---

1   [Browne], "Later From Utah," Dispatch, August 5, 1858, *New-York Tribune*, September 6, 1858; correspondent of St. Louis *Democrat* quoted in *Hawk Eye* (Burlington, Iowa), December 7, 1858, and in *New York Times*, November 19, 1858.

Judge Eckels' Indian servant as a boy ("Tom") without identified tribal affiliation, whereas in 1858 a St. Louis newspaperman had offered this information: "[Judge Eckels] has with him a female Pi-Utah Indian, about eleven years of age, named Mary Tecumbiats, whom he rescued some time ago from a band of starving Utes, who were about to kill the girl for the purpose of regaling themselves on her flesh. She is a black-haired, fat, and clumsy specimen of the female gender."² What Browne intended to accomplish with these character transformations is unclear, but they were not accidental.

If Browne provided little information in his 1858 dispatches of a personal nature about Henrietta Polydore, he was not much more forthcoming about Judge Eckels. It was an odd reticence since he had traveled and lived at close quarters with Eckels since their days spent attending lynchings in Leavenworth City, Kansas Territory, during August 1857. Largely missing from Browne's published work of 1858 and 1877, then, was a picture of the hostility, if not personal animosity, that had developed between the judge and the Latter-day Saints since the fall of 1857, long before they came in contact with one another. On the day Judge Eckels approached Salt Lake City under the protection of the army—only five weeks before the Polydore case was to arrive in his court room—an eastbound mail coach passed him on the trail bearing a mass petition to President Buchanan urging removal of Eckels and three other federal appointees.

In a cover letter transmitting this remarkable document on behalf of Brigham Young and sixty other petitioners, Governor Cumming explained, "All the gentlemen whose names are mentioned in the Petition are unusually obnoxious to the People of this territory and in my opinion ought to be promptly removed from their respective offices." The petition itself elaborated on Cumming's recommendation:

---

2   [Unattributed], "Arrival of Celebrities from Salt Lake City," Dispatch, St. Louis *Democrat*, November 16, 1858, reprinted in *New York Times*, ibid.

Chief Justice Eckels, while yet en route to this Territory expressed himself in most vindictive and prejudiced terms against the people of the Territory. Contrary to Law and the established principles of Constitutional justice, he summoned a Grand Jury of the attaches and followers of the Army [at Camp Scott], and before them did himself cause testimony to be presented and Indictments found (for most serious offences.) against numerous citizens of the United States, residents of the Territory. He has himself acted as Judge, Prosecutor, and Clerk, of his own Court, and has ever during his residence in the Territory, used not only his personal, but Judicial influence to provoke a collision and disturbances between the people of the Territory and the Federal Government. Though often invited, and assurances of safety and protection given, he has refused to come into our settlements or separate himself from the Army up till this time.

As the summer unfolded, more invective followed, this time alleging sexual peccadilloes.[3]

In this section the author also introduces us to Marshal Peter K. Dotson's new, court-ordered role as Henrietta's temporary guardian and that of Browne and interim U.S. Attorney Washington Jay McCormick—Henry Polydore's proxy attorneys—as Dotson's unofficial assistants. With this arrangement in place from a literary standpoint, the reader understands for the first time the meaning of

---

3   Gov. Alfred Cumming to Sec. of Sate Lewis Cass, June 26, 1858, Alfred Cumming Papers, Rubenstein Library, Duke University, Durham, N.C., microfilm copy at Utah State Historical Society; Petition: Citizens of Utah to James Buchanan, June 25, 1858, Thomas L. Kane Papers, Yale Collection of Western Americana, Beinecke Library. Both documents are discussed in MacKinnon, ed., *At Sword's Point, Part 2*, 571–80 and 635–39, as an early gambit in Brigham Young's efforts to maximize local control over Utah's affairs during her post-war period of "Reconstruction." The petition urged Buchanan to appoint as Eckels' successor Maj. Seth M. Blair of the Nauvoo Legion, a Latter-day Saint and friend of U.S. senator Sam Houston of Texas, who in 1850 had secured Blair's appointment as Utah's first U.S. attorney. See also Thomas G. Alexander, "Carpetbaggers, Reprobates, and Liars: Federal Judges and the Utah War (1857–58)," *The Historian* 70 (Summer 2008): 209–38.

WASHINGTON JAY McCORMICK (1835–1889),
UTAH'S ACTING U.S. ATTORNEY
A young Indiana lawyer-protege of Judge Eckels,
he prosecuted the lawsuit for Henrietta's father
that resulted in her repatriation to England
after brief service as one of her three temporary
guardians in Utah. Photo (1854). *Courtesy Mansfield
Library, University of Montana.*

Browne's somewhat opaque title for his novella, The Ward of the
Three Guardians.

*The author's description in this section of his convoluted ride from
Salt Lake City to the Utah Expedition's new headquarters at Camp
Floyd southwest of Salt Lake City was based on the detailed travelogue he wrote in his July 15, 1858, dispatch to the* Tribune. *In that
piece, Browne stated the purpose of his trip was to "pass a day or two
with some friends and then return." Since the Polydore case would
not arrive in the Utah court system until July 31, it is impossible for
Browne's ramble to Camp Floyd to have been for the purpose later
stated in* Ward—*to consult the lieutenant colonel's wife about appropriate day-to-day supervision for Henrietta.[4] This unnamed lady was
Louisa Hawkins Canby of Kentucky and Indiana, wife of the Tenth
U.S. Infantry's Brevet Lt. Col. Edward R. S. Canby. Accordingly,
the editors believe that the "consultation" at Camp Floyd described
in* Ward *was fictive, a literary device that enabled Browne to bring
Mrs. Canby's widely admired qualities into Henrietta's story on an*

---

4   [Browne], "Utah," Dispatch, July 15, 1858, *New-York Tribune,* August 13, 1858.

anonymous basis. If any woman played a Mother-of-the-Regiment role within the Utah Expedition, it was Louisa ("Lou") Canby.[5]

The Camp Floyd that Browne visited briefly was not the enormous, sprawling adobe establishment of the same name described in most Utah War studies—the second largest community in Utah. Rather it was a temporary cantonment of tents established on July 8 at the north end of Cedar Valley on a bench of the Oquirrh Mountains near Utah Lake's northwest corner. Later called "Old Camp Floyd" or "the Upper Camp," General Johnston abandoned this bivouac in early September of 1858 because of its inadequate water supply and cramped dimensions. With more comfortable adobe quarters built farther south in Cedar Valley during the summer and fall using hired Mormon labor, Johnston was able to avoid the onerous prospect of a second Utah winter in tents.[6]

Browne's introduction here of the notion that Jane Mayer Richards was disillusioned with Mormonism and covertly scheming with Judge

---

5   John Parker Hawkins, *Memoranda Concerning Some Branches of the Hawkins Family and Connections* (Indianapolis: n. pub., 1913), 27. After the Civil War, an army officer who had served with the Canbys at Camp Scott and seen Louisa's volunteer work with the post's hospital, wrote "You may imagine, Messrs. Editors, that a good many of those rough old soldiers [in hospital], who had not seen the smiling face of a mother, sister or any kindred, for a number of years, showered blessings on that excellent lady." [Unattributed], "Gen. Canby," Letter to Editor, *Daily Sentinel* (Raleigh, N.C.), September 11, 1867, 1. In 1859, when Browne wrote from Boston to the post trader at Fort Bridger to reminisce about their Utah War experiences, he asked, "If Col. & Mrs. Canby are still at Bridger I wish that you would mention me to them and convey my respects." Browne to William A. Carter, October 22, 1859, William Alexander Carter Correspondence, 1859–1872, Accn 2496, Box 1, Special Collections, Marriott Library, University of Utah.

6   Duane A. Bylund, *In Search of Johnston's Army: Old Camp Floyd and West Creek as Seen through the Eyes of a Relic Hunter* (New York: iUniverse, Inc., 2009); Roger B. Nielson, *Roll Call at Old Camp Floyd, Utah Territory: Soldiers of Johnston's Army at the Upper Camp, 8 July to 8 September 1858* (Springville, Ut.: Self published, 2003); Donald R. Moorman, with Gene A. Sessions, *Camp Floyd and the Mormons: The Utah War* (Salt Lake City: University of Utah Press, 1992; reprinted 2005).

Eckels to flee east with Henrietta was dramatic but without founda-tion. With this thought, the author set the stage for his later use of one of the stock elements of anti-Mormon literature of the period—the flight from Utah of apostates (often vulnerable women), usually at night and with sinister church assassins in pursuit.

MISS HENRIETTA PEREGO WAS A BLACK-HAIRED, brown-eyed gypsy, bounding with unconscious health, and not over-grown, for her age, in bulk or stature. Her passion was satis-fied or exhausted by the success of her assault.[7] She listened with evident interest to our discussion of the disposition to be made of her, but refused to reply to any questions, and did not stir again from the chair in which the marshal gently but firmly replaced her until, hearing the decision that we should ask the chief-justice to take care of her, over night, she arose without suggestion, took Dotson's hand, and did not falter or attempt to escape on the way. It seemed as if she made a nice and accurate discrimination between the lawyers and the officer, regarding the attorney and myself as the active agents, and Peter as the passive instrument of her capture. But on better acquaintance I came to doubt whether her character was mature enough to comprehend such a distinc-tion. In most of her phases she was only a reckless child.

At his little cottage we discovered the chief-justice cooking his

---

7   To Browne, Henrietta Polydore may have appeared healthy, but by the 1860s, if not earlier, she was afflicted with tuberculosis or consumption as it was then called. Her aunt Jane also became infected, raising the question of who contracted TB when and from whom.

own supper[8] with the aid of an Indian boy, whom he had begged or bought from a Uinta chief during the previous winter while I was in the States, and had christened Tom. Tom's most prominent feature was a wonderful shock of coarse and brilliant black hair, as thick as the fur of a beaver, which the judge caused to be closely cropped at short intervals. How he and his master first devised their means of communication I never knew. When I returned to the camp [from the East] in May, they possessed a system of exchanging ideas through a combination of pantomime with a gibberish of the Ute and English languages, and the kind old man had made some progress towards instructing Tom, through this obscure medium, in the Christian scheme of salvation.

The object of our visit did not surprise the judge; and he remarked to us, with a dry smile, that he had intended to call at Elder Baxter's cottage after supper to offer the same service which we came to request. During the conversation Tom and Henrietta struck up a familiar acquaintance. The artful reserve of the girl dissipated like a cloud, and soon she substituted herself for the judge in the culinary processes at the fire-place. She also helped to spread the table, and satisfied us by her share in the meal that mental distress had not impaired her appetite. The novel companionship with Tom diverted her thoughts from her past life, if indeed they ever dwelt there seriously at all. Inquiries which I afterwards made about her mode of living in Elder Peckham's family led me to believe that within certain simple limits of restraint she had been free from all instruction, and was more truly at this hour a

---

8   Over the years, Browne was consistently impressed by Eckels' ability to fend for himself. In 1858, he wrote, "I have seen the Chief Justice cutting the turf for a chimney, and punching the oxen which were drawing logs to build his cabin. . . . the civil offices, at least, in connection with the Utah expedition are not sinecures." [Browne], "On the Way to Utah," Dispatch, May 14, 1858, New-York Tribune, June 12, 1858.

child of nature than the Indian boy was after his half year's discipline in the judge's service.[9] Tom made up a bed for her, of skins and blankets, in the corner of a pantry that led out of the kitchen. Then in the kitchen he made a similar bed for himself; and before we left the cottage the two children were sound asleep.

The marshal and the attorney walked back with me to Elder Baxter's, and there upon the western veranda, where just a week ago the latter had tossed me the general's dispatches, we resumed consideration of the serious problem what to do with this extraordinary child. The more we considered it the more difficult it appeared. Our hasty and efficient response to the general's appeal to "the benevolence of the legal profession" had got us into a predicament of which I suspect that Mrs. Peckham the fourth was not unconscious when she swept out of the court room on Hosea Stout's arm.

On only one point were we agreed: that was, in cordial imprecations upon Mr. Julian Perego, of St. Albans, Herts, England, for doing his domestic business by proxy. (I must observe here, in justice to us, though I take part of the credit from the record, that during the whole debate no allusion was made to the pecuniary side of the question, although we justly might have reckoned

---

9   In the mid-nineteenth century visitors to Utah as well as settlers expressed concern about indiscipline among the territory's boys, but it is problematic to portray Henrietta Polydore as running wild sequestered in the Richards household. Surrounded by five sister wives, including her own aunt, it is not unreasonable to assume that "Lucy" may have been, if anything, over-supervised. In this connection it is worth noting that on March 19, 1857, the eve of the Utah War, Samuel W. Richards had taken as his fifth wife Ann Jones Cash, his widowed former housekeeper at the British Mission in Liverpool who had emigrated to Utah in 1855 and was living with the Richards family. A descendant-biographer characterized the union as "a convenience marriage only." In 1858 "Auntie Cash" was nearly sixty years old, twenty years older than Samuel and a force with which the Richards children, irrespective of parentage, had to reckon. Maureen Carr Ward, "Samuel Whitney Richards: His Wives, Children, and Descendants," http://www.n1.net/~mcward/swr.htm (accessed August 4, 2002).

it into the account as an aggravation of the embarrassment.[10])
Midnight overtook us with no intelligent plan devised for dis-
posing of our ward. The difficulty was to combine safety with
any decent and adequate provision for her custody and comfort
until we could contrive the means of sending her to Washington.
We separated, agreeing to meet after breakfast and exchange any
ideas which might suggest themselves meanwhile.

I awoke early with a notion about the subject which I proceeded
at once to act upon. The sun was rising when, having succeeded in

---

10 Browne may have been gilding the lily in portraying his role in the Polydore case
as financially selfless and performed on an essentially *pro bono* basis. He and his
co-counsel McCormick sought legal fees and expense reimbursement from Secretary Cass in amounts that sent shock waves through the department of state's
auditors. To cushion the impact of their invoice and justify the decision to return
Henrietta to the Atlantic Coast immediately, Browne and McCormick invoked
considerations of humanity, international relations, and moral turpitude. Writing
of themselves in the third person, they commented that Mr. Polydore's co-counsel
(and Henrietta's guardians) had been "called to go perhaps beyond the line of professional duty towards this client, for they have been prompted (as under similar
circumstances any gentleman would have been,) by motives of humanity and a
desire to promote international good-will. . . . Another reason [for our decision]
is our belief that the mother will return to this city before the expiration of the
summer. We concluded that a longer sojourn in this community would be detri-
mental to the child's morals, and would be against the father's desire. . . . It is too
true that the condition of society in this Territory is so deplorable that the child
would inevitably become a 'spiritual' wife had she been suffered to remain among
the Mormons two years longer." That said, the two attorneys rendered a bill for
"professional services in the case of Henry Polydore vs. Samuel W. Richards and
Jane Mayer" in the amount of $650.00 (more than three times Browne's monthly
salary from the *Tribune* for reporting on the case), while seeking expense reimbursement of $600 for transportation from Salt Lake City to the British Embassy
in Washington for Henrietta and Jane Mayer (described as her "attendant"), and
$299.35 for seventy-nine items of clothing or accessories acquired in a spending
spree to outfit (and probably placate) Henrietta for the trip at the Salt Lake City
store of C. A. Perry & Co., sutler for the Utah Expedition's Tenth Infantry. Browne
and McCormick to Cass, August 10, 1858, Polydore File, U.S. State Department,
Territorial Papers, Utah series, Vol. 1 (April 30, 1853–December 24, 1859), NARA;
also microfilm, FHL 491,567, Church History Library.

opening Dotson's barn and saddling my Indian pony without dis-
turbing his household, I rode under Peter's window and listened
to the snoring of the good man. Everything he did was done so
thoroughly! If I should wake him by calling from the outside at
that hour, so I reasoned, I should risk receiving a shot through
the window. In those days every Gentile in the city slept with
a revolver by his bedside.[11] Scrawling on a slip of paper, by the
uncertain light, *"I've gone to Camp Floyd to see the lieutenant-colonel's wife; the C.J. [Chief Justice] and Tom must take care of the girl
till I get back,"* I pushed it under the window-sash.

By following the great southern road down the valley of the Jordan, the distance to Cedar Valley[12] and Camp Floyd was about
fifty miles; but I had heard of a cut-off, leading up a canyon on
the east and down another on the west of the Oquirrh Mountains,[13] which would shorten the journey one third. So, instead
of following the Jordan southward, I forded the river and rode
towards the Oquirrh range across the arid, level bottom of the
valley. Three villages (or "forts," as the Mormons call them) lay at

11 Browne was not exaggerating about the ubiquity of firearms. The civilians at Camp
Scott were also heavily armed. Mrs. Gov. Cumming assured her sister-in-law in
Georgia, "I am quite safe here—but guns & pistols are as much a part of our tent
furniture as tables or seats," and a camp follower warned Thomas L. Kane, "It
doesn't do to speak too plain on personal matters—here, where every man wears a
revolver." Elizabeth Wells Randall Cumming to Anne Elizabeth Cumming Smith,
April 5, 1858, Alfred Cumming Papers, Rubenstein Library, Duke University;
Thomas L. Kane, "Diary II (1858)," undated entry, 19. Thomas Leiper Kane Papers,
Special Collections, Stanford University Libraries, Stanford University, typed
transcription contained on microfilm, copy at Church History Library.
12 Cedar Valley is west of Utah Lake and about forty miles southwest of Salt Lake
City. The tree called a cedar in Utah was not the majestic one found in the Pacific
Northwest but usually was a scrubby bush more akin to the juniper.
13 The "Oquirrh Mountains have a north-south orientation at the south end of Great
Salt Lake. The mountains used to be heavily wooded but have been deforested by
heavy logging, smelter fumes, and other problems. On the west in Tooele valley."
Van Cott, *Utah Place Names*, 282. In Utah, the range's name has a distinctive pro-
nunciation: "Oaker."

intervals of six or seven miles along the route. They were disconsolate abodes indeed for human creatures. A thick mud wall, surrounded by a ditch so clogged with filth that the thread of water within it seemed to crawl instead of flow, and inclosing a square about three hundred yards in diameter; a row of crumbling adobes and crazy log-cabins abutting on the wall along each side of the esplanade; half a dozen groups of tow-headed children tumbling over one another like puppies at play; a flock of geese, a few sheep closely shorn, and now and then a cow or an ox straying at will; a bronze-faced, hard-fisted woman milking a goat; and here and there a wagon or a tip-cart roasting in the sunshine, with the wheel-tires dropping from the shrunken felloes,—imagine these in the case of one of the forts, and you have the picture of all three. The land around them was entirely incapable of cultivation, for want of water to irrigate it. The only fields inclosed and tilled in this part of the valley lay near the foot of the mountain, along the brooks which flowed down the canyons.

Between the first and second forts my pony cast a shoe, which delayed me at least three hours before I could find a blacksmith to replace it. So it was past one o'clock when I rode under the wall of the third fort and turned into Rose Canyon.[14] The heat was intense, and I was almost choked with the dust which rose from the parched soil at every step. The pony was very tired, and so, being satisfied that I should reach the camp long before sunset, I let him jog slowly, nibbling the tops of the tufts of grass which sometimes were so tall that they nodded above the horn of my Mexican saddle. Wherever a scythe could get a fair sweep between the road and the alders which skirted the babbling brook, the Mormons had been mowing, and in a little while I met a wagon laden with the hay and surrounded by half a dozen

---

14   Rose Canyon, located near Herriman, Utah, was often covered with wildflowers
      (https://www.alltrails.com/trail/us/utah/rose-canyon-spring-trail).

saints on horseback, who eyed me curiously. Desiring to confirm my belief that I was in Rose Canyon, I asked them whether I was on the right road to reach Cedar Valley and the soldiers' camp across the mountain. After a brief consultation behind the hay-cart, their leader informed me civilly that I was not, and told me to turn back and take the next canyon to the north; and they were kind enough to detail one of their number to show me the way. I was cordial in my thanks to the young man, who rode with me across the slopes at least a mile to insure my making no mistake. My sense of obligation was so great that I even lent him my pocket-flask and a plug of tobacco, the first of which he returned to me half empty, and the second he did not return at all. Bidding him a friendly good-by, I trotted into the canyon which he pointed out, pausing only for a moment to cut a switch from a scrub oak, with which I urged the pony into a gallop, while I recalled to mind the New Year's pie and speculated on what the lieutenant-colonel would give me to-day for dinner.

At last it occurred to me that I had been riding quite long enough to have turned the summit of the ridge, according to every description of the route which had been given me in the city. The flowering shrubs around were very fragrant, and the brook was noisy and cooling, and the scenery very picturesque; but I was not diverted so far from the aim of the journey as to forget to look at my watch. That told me it was already four o'clock, and still I was jogging along upon the ascent. The road dwindled into a wood-trail, with faint signs of wagon tracks; this narrowed into a horse-path; and that disappeared among the grass under a clump of pine-trees. I had been ascending abruptly for two or three miles, and now, a few hundred yards above my head, I could see specks of snow along the rocky edge of the ridge which sharply cut the sky. The sun was setting when the pony stood on the summit, knee-deep in a snow-drift, and from his back I could look down three or four thousand feet—not into Cedar Valley. I believe that I should be pardoned here and hereafter for any disrespectful remarks about my obliging Mormon friends which I might have made had anybody been present to hear them.

There was no alternative but to descend the mountain by the same path by which I had climbed it. Between nine and ten o'clock, by the light of a waning moon, I reached a farm-house on the plain, where I was hospitably received by a saint whose family already had gone to bed. It consisted of two wives and seven children, and the whole household occupied a single room. He gave me a ragged but clean quilt for a covering, and I stretched myself upon the floor with my saddle for a pillow. Pony fared better than his master, for he was picketed within reach of an ample meal of fresh hay. I fell asleep while my host (who, notwithstanding the warmth of the night, was sweltering in a feather-bed) struggled with an argument intended to convince me that the North American Indians are the lost tribes of Israel. The discourse was interspersed with pithy pieces of advice and warning to the two older boys, who got into a fight in bed, and with lamentations over the bad prospects of the crops. In justice to the old man I must add that he was perfectly sincere, and that according to his means he treated me very kindly. His charge the next morning for entertaining me and pony was twelve and one half cents. I put a gold dollar into his hand, and he put it into his pocket before either of his wives could catch a glimpse of it, and blessed me fervently and prayed that I yet might be gathered into the fold by the Good Shepherd. Then I rode away into the canyon from which I had been turned back the previous afternoon, and reached the lieutenant-colonel's quarters before breakfast.[15]

---

15   This account of Browne's trip to Camp Floyd was derived from [Browne], "Utah. Going to Camp. Misdirected by the Saints," Dispatch, July 15, 1858, to New-York Tribune, August 13, 1858.

The scenery of Cedar Valley was enchanting. On every side but the southeast it was encompassed by steep mountains; but there, across a broad interval, the eye could follow for fifty miles the snowy ridge of the Wasatch range. In a gap between the hills in the foreground glimmered the blue basin of Lake Utah. Dense groves of the trees which gave their name to the valley skirted its entire circumference. Near one of these groves the camp was pitched, and almost every tent was prefaced with a bower of cedar branches, and carpeted with the fragrant twigs. The general might have fancied himself Judas Maccabaeus keeping the Feast of the Tabernacles with the Jewish army.[16] The dust, however, was almost intolerable when it was raised by petty tempests, which came nobody knew whence, and blew nobody knew where, at any and every hour of the day.[17] As I rode up to the lieutenant-colonel's tent, one of these provoking gusts swept away the cloth with which the servants were laying the table for breakfast in the bower, and whirled it against pony's head and shoulders, so that, seizing it, I was able to present myself to its mistress and beg for hospitality and counsel under a flag of truce.

Breakfast over, I stated the case which was perplexing the guardians of our English waif, and found, to my delight, that I had not counted in vain upon the clear insight and sound sense of this excellent lady.[18]

"The girl," she said, "is amused today by her new playmate. But

16　The Maccabees, led by their forceful leader Judas, successfully rebelled against the Seleucid Empire—liberating Jerusalem and purifying Herod's Temple. Browne may have felt "the general" saw himself as similarly freeing Utah from religious oppression.

17　The dust storms and whirlwinds plagued the troops at Camp Floyd to an extent that they dubbed them "Johnsoons" in honor of their commander who had selected Cedar Valley as their bivouac.

18　This session with Mrs. Canby was wholly fictional.

to-morrow she will sorrow for her aunt, and become unmanageable. My advice is that you make friends with the aunt and give the child to her charge until you can send her East. If she has any genuine affection for the child she will undertake the charge—especially if you can pay her for her trouble; and if she does possess the influence you say over Mr. Peckham, he, being a man of substance, can be persuaded by her to give you security that the child shall not be lost or come to harm. What kind of security it shall be is a matter for you lawyers to determine. I think that under the circumstances the father will have no just cause to complain of such a risk. If this plan is not practicable, bring the child here to the camp. I will not engage to take care of her myself, but I will promise to find some one here to lodge her safely and comfortably. I know one of the sergeant's wives whom I could trust with her; but I do not hesitate to advise adopting the first course, if it is possible, for the sake of the child's own happiness."

When pony turned the corner from Main Street in Salt Lake City late that night, I knew by two little specks of fire which were glowing upon the veranda of Elder Baxter's cottage that the marshal and the attorney were smoking there as usual and awaiting my return. Indeed, they had been waiting in that very place ever since sunset. The diagnosis of the case by the lieutenant-colonel's wife was perfect. During the day Miss Henrietta had quarreled with Tom, and after that had behaved as ill as possible, slapping, kicking, and even biting every one within her reach. About nine o'clock Tom had come over to Dotson's with a message from the judge that she had cried herself to sleep.

When I made my report it was voted by our council that the lieutenant-colonel's wife possessed more common sense than the whole bench and bar of Utah Territory, and the marshal was deputed to enter into immediate negotiations with Jane Moore.

She proved to be a person of strong common sense, although the fact of her conversion to Mormonism would be conclusive to the contrary with unreflecting persons. How a woman of her intelligence and good manners, used to all the best associations of the English middle classes, ever came into her relation to Elder Peckham was and still is to me a puzzle. In the days that followed, I opened the door more than once for an explanation of the mystery, but she always avoided a disclosure. She received the marshal amiably, avowed a sincere acquiescence in the decree of the court for the return of the child to the father, pledged her word to enter into no conspiracy or combination with the mother (who, she told us, had also become a Mormon), and expressed not merely a willingness but an earnest desire to relieve us from our difficult position by taking care of the child in our behalf and inducing Elder Peckham to give security for its safety, although, she said, it doubtless would be necessary to make a liberal provision for the maintenance of the child, in order to gain his consent.

When Dotson repeated this conversation to us, such a complete and instantaneous compliance with our wishes seemed suspicious. It was explained, however, by something which occurred the next day, although we did not know of that until long afterwards. Under pretext of coming to console Miss Henrietta, whose active demonstrations of anger had now subsided into sullenness, Jane Moore procured a private interview with the chief-justice, in which she told him that she loathed her condition and besought his secret aid to enable her to escape from Utah.[19] The plan for her relief did not suggest itself at once, but was developed in

---

19   As discussed above, there is no reason to accept Browne's description of Jane's motives as anything but fiction. All indications are that she traveled east solely to care for her niece Henrietta and perhaps to visit her mother and Mayer siblings in Arkansas, whom she had not seen since 1854.

connection with the means we adopted later for sending Henrietta to Washington. Meanwhile she served us as a useful ally, although not possessing the real clew to her conduct, I confess that for a long while I never trusted her completely. Her very astuteness in our interest inspired me with a fear that she was enticing our favor with a sinister purpose. No piece of diplomacy could be more adroit, rapid, or successful than her persuasion of Peckham within forty-eight hours to give us a bond bearing the names of Brigham Young and Heber Kimball and several other wealthy Mormons as sureties, in a very large sum (I think it was as much as $30,000), for the safe keeping of the child, who was thereupon returned to her care, to the great sorrow of Tom, with whom she had become very friendly again.[20]

One of the stipulations of the arrangement was that the marshal, the attorney, and myself should have free access to Henrietta at all times, and accordingly one of us visited Peckham's house every day to make sure that no harm should befall our ward. By slow degrees her animosity against the attorney and myself (she never, from the first, showed any against Dotson) changed to mere shyness, and then that disappeared and we became good friends. In the course of these visits it became known to all of us at last, in some insensible way, that Jane Moore desired to escape from her Mormon associations. I do not remember any one conversation in which she told us so, and our knowledge did not come from the chief-justice. He never mentioned her secret interview with him until the moment when it became possible for us to aid her flight.

---

20   There was no such bond, and there are no signs that Brigham Young or Heber C. Kimball—both burdened during the summer of 1858 with more global concerns—took an interest in the Polydore case.

1856 Utah Territorial Census for Salt Lake City
listing Henrietta Polydore by her alias "Lucy." *Courtesy of Family Search.*

SECTION V.

"An Unexpected Deliverance
Had Come"

ROAD TRIP HOME

🌿 EDITORIAL NOTES

In this penultimate section of Ward, *Albert Browne again drew heavily on first-hand knowledge but continued fabricating material for dramatic effect or to bridge gaps in his knowledge of Henrietta's return to the Atlantic Coast. The fact is Browne knew little about what she experienced after leaving Salt Lake City on September 15, 1858, with Judge Eckels, aunt Jane and her infant son Phineas, and a few families of English refugee-apostates. Since Browne's last dispatch for the* Tribune *was dated October 8, everything he wrote for* Ward's *last two sections drew on his memory or imagination rather than his invaluable personal scrapbook of press clippings.*

Perhaps most intriguing about this fifth section is what it omitted. Among the missing material was Judge Eckels' tale of pursuit for five hundred miles by a band of "Danites," ecclesiastical assassins who, real or not, appeared in the obligatory chase scene found in virtually every Victorian melodrama about Mormon Utah. Eckels first expressed alarm about such a danger in his report of November 11 to Secretary of State Cass from Fort Leavenworth, Kansas Territory, the army post closest to the end-of-telegraph at Boonville, Missouri.

Improbable as Eckels' story was, he repeated it to newspaper reporters the next day.[1] *Browne, of course, implied such a threat by describing*

---

1   The editors believe there was no pursuit of Eckels' party by Mormon "Danites." Eckels made no reference to such danger two times when he most logically would have done so: when meeting with William A. Carter at Fort Bridger on September 26; and when writing to Secretary Cass from the Big Sandy River on October 2. Fantasies of a 500-mile pursuit across the plains most likely arose in the judge's mind a little later in October and farther east—at Fort Laramie, where Eckels encountered not the fact of such a chase but the over-active imagination of a bored frontier garrison. By the time Eckels and Henrietta reached Washington in early December, the capital correspondent of the *New York Times* was reporting, "When the Judge arrived at Fort Laramie, on his way to the States, with Miss Polydore in charge, he learned that a party of Danites,—several of whom were known to be in Salt Lake City when he left,—had been inquiring for him, having unquestionably pursued him with a view of forcibly abducting the child." There is no evidence that Brigham Young or his "b'hoys" took any interest in the Polydore case during August 1858 or thereafter. To the contrary, as discussed below, there are signs that at about this time Young's focus was not on preventing Henrietta's departure from Samuel Richards' household but rather was on resolving his suspicions about Richards' problematic financial stewardship at the British Mission earlier in the decade.

The Department of State logged in receipt of this letter from Eckels to Cass dated Fort Leavenworth, November 11, 1858, with the terse summary, "Is bringing back Henrietta Polydore. Has been followed by Mormons more than 500 miles." Before the consolidation of government records at the new National Archives in the 1930s, this letter and its summary were filed in State's bureau of rolls and libraries per David W. Parker, *Calendar of Papers in Washington Archives Relating to the Territories of the United States (to 1873)*, Pub. No. 148 (Washington: Carnegie Institution, 1911), 400 (Item #8069). With NARA's creation, this letter should have come to rest in General Records, Dept. of State, Domestic Letters, Vol. 48, RG 59, but on January 30, 2009, NARA archivist Joseph D. Schwarz notified MacKinnon by email message that he was "unable to locate this letter." A summary of Eckels' encounter with Carter appears in William A. Carter (Fort Bridger) to Mary E. Carter (Columbia, Mo.), September 26, 1858, typescript of 1955 (p. 18), William A. Carter Papers; Eckels (Big Sandy River) to Cass, October 2, 1858, Polydore case correspondence, U.S. State Department, Territorial Papers, Utah series, Vol. 1, April, 30, 1853–December 24, 1859, National Archives, film #491, 567, Church History Library; "News by Telegraph from Washington," December 6, 1858, *New York Times*, December 7, 1858. For Young's concerns about Richards' financial stewardship, see Epilogue below.

Browne's omission from his novella of such a melodramatic threat to Henrietta is all the more puzzling when one considers how much the American and British

in Ward *the elaborate precautions taken by Eckels' party to conceal their first campsite after leaving Salt Lake City and Jane's surreptitious 2:00 A.M. arrival there. After that early hint of pursuit, Browne dropped further discussion of Henrietta's cross-country travels. Omission of a Danite chase from* Ward *was either a dramatic opportunity missed by Browne-as-novelist or his implicit recognition that Judge Eckels' powers of imagination exceeded reality.*

The second omission worth noting was Browne's failure to mention that the judge's eastbound entourage included seventeen-year-old Elizabeth Cotton, another English convert attempting to return home after several years in Utah. Cotton, a native of Ardsley, South Yorkshire, had traveled to Iowa in 1856 and then gone to Utah with an uncle and aunt in the Hunt wagon train immediately to the rear of the ill-fated Willie and Martin handcart companies. Badly shaken by this near-death experience, Cotton suffered another blow upon discovering that Mormonism in Utah was far different than the religion represented to her by missionaries in England. On February 1, 1858, Elizabeth wrote her mother to describe her disillusionment, the seamy side of polygamy, and her intent to abandon Mormonism for home. Publication of Cotton's titillating letter created a sensation first in England and then throughout the United States, while confirming Henry Polydore's anxiety about his own daughter's jeopardy. What followed in short order, of course, was the army's arrival in the Salt Lake Valley, the Polydore court case, Elizabeth Cotton's plea for Judge

public thrived on such tales of peril—real or imagined. A good example of such fare was a course of lectures titled "Utah and the Mormons" delivered in Baltimore's Temperance Temple by sixteen-year-old Helen M. Dresser, a waif who supposedly "escaped" from Utah in 1857 after a three-year residence in the Salt Lake Valley under ambiguous circumstances. Tickets for Miss Dresser's lectures were twenty-five cents and were accompanied by appropriate musical numbers sung by the presumably all-male "Apollonians." See "Lectures on Utah and the Mormons," Baltimore *Daily Exchange*, May 16, 1859, 1/6.

Eckels' protection, and her departure from Utah with him in a cloud of controversy.[2]

Why did Ward *step over the fact that Cotton had traveled east with Eckels? The editors believe Browne may have done so because of his recollection that in 1858 the judge was beset by perceptions of sexual improprieties by the Latter-day Saint hierarchy and even the Utah Expedition's troops.*[3] *Editorially deleting Elizabeth Cot-*

---

2   Elizabeth Cotton (Utah) to Mother (Barnsley, South Yorkshire, England), February 1, 1858, reprinted from Leeds [England] *Mercury* as "A Picture of Life Among the Mormons" in Cardiff and Merthyr [Wales] *Guardian*, May 8, 1858, 7/2. A reprinted but truncated version of Elizabeth's letter appeared in American newspapers within a month, as with "What an English Girl Thinks of the Mormons," Mt. Vernon, Ohio *Democratic Banner*, June 1, 1858, 1/6.

3   While it was clear that Judge Eckels was indignant about Mormon plural marriage, there were perceptions in Utah by both non-Mormons and Latter-day Saints that he was not above reproach, if not a womanizer. Several incidents come to mind. On June 11, 1858, Capt. John W. Phelps of the Fourth U.S. Artillery journalized about a drunken spree at Camp Scott on the eve of the Utah Expedition's departure from winter quarters for its march on the Salt Lake Valley. It was a bacchanalia that Captain Phelps recorded with a mixture of amazement and disgust: "The order is out for the move. . . . Several drunken soldiers of the 10th Inf[antr]y got into a row against Judge Eckels at his [quarters] today. One of them struck him and the Clerk of the Court several times. The judge has had some womenfolk at his establishment who are probably at the bottom of the affair." Captain Phelps' contemporaneous comments are consistent with the old-age recollections of Lt. William R. R. Stowell, a Nauvoo Legionnaire held captive at Camp Scott during the winter of 1857–58: "About this time I received a present from a Mrs. Wordsworth . . . She had a niece [Elizabeth Cotton] with her and it was well understood in camp that Judge Eckels share[d] his bed with her." Sergeant John Rozsa of the U.S. Tenth Infantry verified that Cotton was indeed at Camp Scott that winter working as a seamstress and laundress, and that he had unsuccessfully proposed marriage to her.

Two months later, on August 12, after the army had passed through Salt Lake City and was building Camp Floyd, Eckels wrote to 2d Lt. Clarence E. Bennett, adjutant of the Tenth Infantry, to report a lack of success in obtaining for him a suitable "bedfellow for the coming winter" but pledged to keep on trying. This letter was found on the road to Camp Floyd by a Mormon and duly sent by the church's leaders to the Buchanan administration in support of ongoing efforts to have Eckels recalled as biased and unfit for his assignment. From Salt Lake City Apostle John

ton in Ward *from Judge Eckels' entourage was a way for Browne to avoid entangling Henrietta's story with the controversy over Cotton's apostasy and the seamy behavior surrounding her sojourn in Utah. Simultaneously it lowered the judge's profile as a person frequently surrounded by attractive women, especially since Elizabeth Cotton had been described by another reporter as "young and beautiful— just such a one as would be likely to be pestered immediately on her arrival in the City of the Saints, by the tender attentions of a score or two of its gallant polygamous gentry." In 1877 Browne may also have been aware of an additional complexity—that Elizabeth Cotton did not return to England in 1858 but instead became a member of the judge's household in Greencastle, Indiana, where she married his son, William, immediately after his divorce in 1863. A similar concern about image and perceptions may have prompted Browne to change*

Taylor confided to another apostle absent in the East, "the history of the judges is still fraught with much difficulty here. Judge Eckels of Bridger notoriety, if report speaks truly, was engaged while in the very honorable occupation of pimp, for some of the army officers, or some lost letter has belied him, wherein he is made to say to one of his customers, 'that if the lady in question was not exactly what the bill called for, it was nevertheless as well as he could do at present.'" The judge never disavowed the letter, and Lieutenant Bennett later resigned his commission when he married a Mormon actress performing at Camp Floyd amid accusations/perceptions by his brother officers that he was a bigamist.

Hence when Eckels and his nearly all-female party departed Utah in mid-September, the still-scandalized Apostle Taylor commented, "he took some Ladies with him, how far he protected their virtue is not for me to say." Phelps Diary, June 11, 1858, John Wolcott Phelps Papers, Mss Col 2399, Manuscripts and Archives Division, New York Public Library, with typed transcriptions in Hamilton Gardner Papers, Utah State Historical Society; Stowell (with James Little), A Biographical Sketch of William Rufus Rogers Stowell, typescript (Colonia Juarez, Mexico, January 1893), 30, www.familysearch.org accessed September 7, 2020; Eckels to Bennett, August 12, 1858, and "J. T." [John Taylor] to George [Q. Cannon], January 12, 1859, both Yale Collection of Western Americana, Beinecke Library; John Rozsa "Autobiography" (MS 15389) and "Reminiscences" (MS 1877), both Church History Library.

the gender of the person he described as the judge's young Paiute servant-mascot from female ("Mary") to male ("Indian Tom").[4]

Perhaps the novella's most obvious omission related to the Mormon Move South, Brigham Young's evacuation of Salt Lake City and northern Utah during March–July 1858 and preparations to incinerate its infrastructure in anticipation of the army's arrival in the Salt Lake Valley. It was part of Young's Russian-style scorched earth policy[5] and southbound exodus toward Mexico involving an estimated 30,000 people—the greatest mass movement of civilian refugees in North America since the flight of British Loyalists to Canada during the American Revolution. In alluding in Ward *to "Jane Moore's" travel from Salt Lake City to Provo, Browne implied obliquely that*

---

4   A glimpse into the extent to which Elizabeth Cotton's proximity to Judge Eckels raised controversy appears in Captain Phelps' diary. Phelps and his artillery battery encountered a hard-drinking Eckels on the trail south of Salt Lake City three days after the Utah Expedition marched through the city in search of a site for its permanent garrison. In tow with Eckels, whom he knew from their winter together at Camp Scott, were Cotton, her apostate uncle and aunt (the Wadsworths from Yorkshire), Paiute Mary, and a Nicaraguan freebooter who had spent the winter imprisoned by Brigham Young in Salt Lake City. Phelps recorded: "I called to see Judge Eckels, the Chief Justice of Utah Territory. It was close to my camp, and his lodging place was between two wagons. This was his only enclosure or shelter. . . . the clouds of dust that dimmed the sun had made the Judge as black as the rest of us. . . . he arose to meet me, and while offering a bottle of whiskey for our consolation introduced to us 'Col. Fabens of the Nicaraguan Army' . . . Taken altogether it was one of the most wretched spectacles that I ever witnessed. What a mixture of dust, Mormonism, jurisprudence, whiskey and filibusterism! And to be met with here in the Rocky Mountains!" Capt. John W. Phelps, Diary, June 29, 1858, transcription courtesy of Mr. Jeffrey N. Walker, Salt Lake City.

5   "Young was well aware that Sebastopol, a Crimean port city on the Black Sea, had figured prominently during the recently concluded Crimean War. British, French, and Ottoman forces, commanded by Lord Raglan, laid siege to the city of Sebastopol for more than a year (1854–55). When it became apparent to Sebastopol's Russian defenders that the city would be lost, they burned the entire city rather than surrender it to their enemies." Kenneth L. Alford, " 'We have now the Territory on wheels': Direct and Collateral Costs of the 1858 Move South," *Journal of Mormon History* 45, no. 2 (2019): 96.

perhaps Jane Mayer Richards and Henrietta Polydore had participated in the Move South. If they did, such an upheaval would have
been Henrietta's greatest adventure in Utah, one that did not run
its course until shortly before the focus on her future shifted to Judge
Eckels' Salt Lake City courtroom.[6]

The overwhelming likelihood is that during March–April 1858 the
Richards household—five sister wives and a substantial number of
children (including Jane, Phineas, and Henrietta)—did indeed flee
south even without the help of Samuel Richards, then en route to Utah
from England. Such involvement is what Elder Richards would have
expected based on the guidance he provided Jane from the distance of
Liverpool less than three months before the Move South started:

> I often think of home with anxious feelings, not knowing what may be
> the movements there, consequently feel quite unable to give you such
> advice as might be best for the family but I would say to you all, make
> yourselves acquainted with the general counsels of the [First] Presi-
> dency and seek to carry them out to the best of your ability. If it is to
> cache grain, do so. If it is to burn houses and everything else, do that.
> & all of you my dear family I hope will be ready in your feelings for
> anything that may be required to build up and defend the Kingdom
> of God upon the earth. This is our mission to this world and let us
> [ful]fill it in the best possible manner, seeking the happiness of each
> other and the glory of God.[7]

As Brigham Young announced the Move South on March 21, Marietta S. Calkin, plural wife of Samuel W. Richards' successor at the

---

6   Richard D. Poll, "The Move South," BYU Studies 29 (Fall 1989): 65–88; Kenneth L.
     Alford, "We have now the Territory on Wheels," Journal of Mormon History 45,
     no. 2 (2019): 92–114; MacKinnon, "Blessed Be Nothing: The Mormon Move South,"
     in At Sword's Point, Part 2, 309–45, and "Exodus and the Utah War: Tales from the
     Mormon Move South, 1858," Overland Journal, Quarterly of the Oregon-California
     Trails Association 34 (Fall 2016): 89–100.

7   Samuel W. Richards to Jane Mayer Richards, January 1, 1858, Samuel W. Richards
     Papers, MS 6576, Box 1, Fd 13, Church History Library.

British Mission, lacked guidance from her absent husband, Asa. On her own initiative Mrs. Calkin wrote Young, "I would like to tell you how strong we are to move or help ourselves. . . . looking glasses and clocks might as well be burned at once as to be put indifferently away— and I prefer it,—For I could then say 'blessed be nothing.'" Months later, overburdened and suffering from smallpox, Asa Calkin wrote to one of Marietta's sister wives: "So, you have pulled up bag and baggage and left my house while I have gone have you? Well, how do you like 'Mormonism' rough and tumble? . . . Only hold on to this rod of iron and it will land you safe on the other side. 'The Kingdom of God or nothing' is the motto, hold on to it and it well help you on wonderfully."[8]

Why none of this drama made it into Browne's story is another of the mysteries associated with how he chose to write Ward in 1877.

Finally, it should be noted that this fifth section of Ward raises the question of when A. G. Browne last saw Henrietta Polydore. Taken at face value, the novella leads readers to believe that their farewell was on September 16, as Judge Eckels' party broke camp after its first night in the Wasatch. By this scenario, Browne's awareness of "the rest of Henrietta's story" came from two letters supposedly written by Judge Eckels from Washington in early November 1858 and received by Browne in Massachusetts upon his own return from Utah. That is not what happened in terms of substance or timing. An examination of the Browne family's voluminous papers at Harvard yields no such letters from the judge. From his interview with the Democrat in St. Louis, we know that an eastbound Browne passed Eckels' slower-moving party along the Oregon Trail in Kansas Territory. It is inconceivable that Browne would not have stopped at least briefly to exchange

8   Samuel W. Richards to Jane Mayer Richards, January 1, 1858, Samuel W. Richards Papers; Marietta S. Calkin to Brigham Young, March 22, 1858, Brigham Young Collection; and Asa S. Calkin to Lizzie Calkin, July 5, 1858, Asa S. Calkin Journal, MS 8138, all Church History Library.

travel information with the judge and pay his respects to Jane and Henrietta. From his mother's diary, we also know that Albert arrived home in Salem just before Thanksgiving and that he immediately went on to the British legation in Washington to, as Mrs. Browne phrased it, "restore to the British Government his young client from Utah, Miss Polydore."[9]

In Washington, Browne surely heard from Judge Eckels the full story of their trek across the Rockies and Great Plains and train travel to the capital from St. Louis via Greencastle. This timing would also have allowed ample opportunity for Browne to see Henrietta before her departure from Washington with a Royal Messenger for New York to take ship for Liverpool on December 8. Consequently, the likelihood is that Albert Browne last saw his "ward" at Lord Napier's diplomatic residence rather than at a bivouac along the Mormon Trail northeast of Salt Lake City two months earlier.

THUS THE SUMMER WORE AWAY. WE HAD WRITTEN to Mr. Perego immediately upon the recovery of the child, but in those days four months was the ordinary interval between the dispatch of a letter to England and the receipt of a reply. We had written also to the British minister at Washington, but September drew towards its close without our hearing from him. We learned afterwards that he forwarded the letter to his home government, and awaited its communication to Mr. Perego and formal instructions thereupon before answering us. No opportunity for sending the child East with a suitable escort had presented itself.

---

9   Sarah Smith Cox Browne, Diary, November 30, 1858, Browne Family Papers, MC 298, Schlesinger Library, Radcliffe Institute.

The Three Guardians of Miss Henrietta (for thus the marshal, the attorney, and myself had come to be styled by our little Gentile community) were again in consultation one star-lit Sunday evening on the veranda where so many of the scenes in this history were acted. Elder Baxter and the two Mrs. Baxters were silent. Their sacred melodies ceased with the harvesting of the crops. A cool breeze was blowing a suggestion of the coming winter down from the snow-clad mountain tops. Henrietta was the topic of our conversation, and we were agreed that unless some lucky chance should soon occur, it would be necessary to keep the child until spring, for it would not be reasonable to expose her to the hardship of a journey across the plains after the wintry weather had set in. Just then the flickering light of a lantern advanced down the yard, shining on the glossy head of Indian Tom, who was its bearer. He never could be made to wear a cap, although he readily adapted himself to trousers and a shirt and jacket. Behind him trudged the chief-justice. The hour of an unexpected deliverance had come.

"My good friends," said the old man, "I find myself of little use in Utah Territory, and I have made up my mind to go back to where I came from,—probably never to return. All of us here are hard-shell democrats, except the doctor yonder, who is the blackest kind of a black republican; yet, black as he is, he cannot think worse than you or I of the doings of our democratic president in this Mormon business. The Utah expedition has been a political and pecuniary swindle from the beginning to the end. I am going to Washington to free my mind on the subject, and it scarcely will be likely that Mr. Buchanan will desire to retain me in his service after he has heard what I have to say. I want to start within a week, and I have a proposal to make about the little English girl. If you will send her East, with her aunt to take care of her, I will furnish the mules and wagon and driver. I shall travel, myself,

in another wagon, with Tom to take care of me. You must provide for the expenses of the girl and her aunt after they reach the
frontier, and I will see them safe to Washington. Mr. Peckham,
as you know, is absent on a journey to the Southern settlements,
and cannot return for a fortnight."

The next Sunday morning two ambulance wagons, each drawn
by an excellent span of mules, rolled out of Salt Lake City, ascended
the bench at the foot of the mountain, and soon disappeared
within the mouth of Emigration Canyon.[10] Tom was the driver of
the first one, and on the seat behind him sat the chief-justice and
Miss Henrietta, among rolls of blankets and packages of cooking
utensils and provisions. I was the driver of the second wagon, and
the marshal and attorney were my companions. At noon we made
a halt for lunch, and then resumed the journey. About four o'clock
in the afternoon we turned the crest of the mountain, and soon
afterwards hauled off from the road into a sheltered ravine, where
we prepared to encamp for the night.

It was a wild and gloomy spot, secure from the sight of any
passers on the road, and while the rest of us unhitched the mules,
Tom and the attorney, first cutting some alder twigs from bushes
that hung over the brook which rattled down the glen towards
the Weber River, walked back and effaced the tracks of the
wagon wheels for some distance from the place where we turned
from the traveled path. After dusk we suffered the fire to burn
low, and sat long around the glowing embers. About two o'clock
we heard the crunching of gravel on the road, as a wagon was
driven cautiously down the descent from the west. Every noise

10   The departure of Eckels and his party for the East was not the furtive exit described
      here. Knowledge of his plans to leave on September 15, 1858, was so widespread that
      a testimonial dinner was tendered to him by Utah's non-Mormon community. This
      invitation and the judge's declension were discussed in the pages of the *Deseret News*.

was audible with startling distinctness, in the dead stillness of the night, above the monotonous rattle of the torrent. The sound ceased for a moment when the wagon reached the point where we ourselves had left the way. Then it was resumed again; and then it changed into a different kind of crunching, as if the team was moving upon turf. Soon the wagon turned the bend in the ravine and approached our camp-fire. Jo Brooks was the driver, and Jane Moore was his passenger.

The Three Guardians of Miss Henrietta reentered Salt Lake City the next afternoon.

Late in October I bade farewell to my two associates, and to Utah altogether, and returned to my home in an Eastern city, which I reached a few weeks before Christmas. I found awaiting me two letters from the chief-justice, which told in a few words the rest of Henrietta's story. In the first letter, dated at Washington, he wrote:—

"I arrived home in Indiana a week ago. Whatever you choose to think of the English girl and her aunt in other respects, I can convince you, when we meet, that they are good campaigners. We were not delayed an hour by either of them, from sickness or any other cause, on the long journey. Jo Brooks parted from us at Leavenworth City. After staying two days with my family (whom, you know, I had not seen for more than a year) I left Tom with them, and came here without any other delay, and within an hour after my arrival I presented Jane Moore and her niece at the British legation. It will amuse you to know that Lord Napier was quite as much embarrassed about the disposition of them as you were. He did not dare to run the risk of putting them at a hotel, and so they had to be kept at the embassy, and really Lady Napier has been excessively kind to them, and has become much interested in the little girl. Mr. Perego has not been heard from. It has been determined not to wait longer for instructions from him, but to send Jane and the girl to England by next Saturday's steamer, under the charge of a queen's messenger. Shortly after our arrival here I received a letter from my wife, with the news that the next day after I left home Mrs. Perego, Henrietta's mother, came there and demanded her child. She appeared here yesterday, and was permitted by Lady Napier to see the child in the presence of Jane and a trusty attendant. I was myself present during a part of the interview. Without going now into details, I believe that Jane is steadfast in the resolve to lead henceforth a worthy life; and Mrs. Perego declares her intention to return to England on the same steamer and seek a reconciliation with her husband; but I mistrust her even more than you did Jane."[11]

I add the next letter entire:—

ASTOR HOUSE, NEW YORK,
November 13, 1858.

MY DEAR DOCTOR,—I have just come from the dock, where I waited until the Cunarder put to sea. By this time she is outside of Sandy Hook. It is a beautiful Indian-summer day, and Jane and Henrietta and her mother, with the gentleman who has the child in his care, stood on deck waving hands and handkerchiefs to me as long as we could see one another.[12] Almost the last words of the child before bidding good-by were a message to you, which she made me promise over and over again to be sure to deliver. "Tell the doctor," said she, "that I said I was *very* sorry that I struck him, and that I wouldn't say that I *was* sorry if I *wasn't*."

---

11   Use of the phrase "a worthy life" for Jane is loaded with cultural assumptions about Mormonism and polygamy, both of which Browne seems to assume she was leaving.

12   As discussed in Section VI, neither Jane nor Judge Eckels were in New York to see Henrietta sail, and Mrs. Polydore was not aboard the *Africa* with her.

U.S. MARSHAL DOTSON'S SALT LAKE CITY HOME,
SETTING FOR PORTIONS OF BROWNE'S NOVELLA

In 1859 Dotson would lose this house following an adverse financial judgment in a lawsuit brought by Brigham Young, an event that prompted him to resign his position, depart Utah, and establish himself as a rancher on an enormous Mexican land grant in Colorado. *Photo (1858) by David A. Burr, courtesy Burr Papers, Kroch Library, Cornell University.*

SECTION VI.

"This Demure Little Lady"

THE TRIUMPH OF FICTION OVER FACT

❦ EDITORIAL NOTES

In this shortest and last of Ward's six sections, author Browne ties a bow to his story while bringing closure to the question of Henrietta Polydore's fate and part of his own. It is Browne's ultimate triumph of fiction over fact.

As the Editors' Epilogue to this study indicates, Browne did not return to Salt Lake City in 1870 for an accidental encounter with Henrietta; he never again traveled farther west than Denver. Henrietta neither married the "square-shouldered, ruddy-faced Englishman" of a type Conan Doyle loved to describe nor sailed off with him into the Pacific sunset of a Joseph Conrad–like New Zealand. Instead, three years before Browne took pen in hand to create such a fantasy, Henrietta died the unpleasant, premature death of a consumptive spinster while visiting her mother in coastal Mississippi.

Whether Browne knew any of this is questionable. The editors believe that he did not. After leaving the ward of the three guardians at the British embassy in Washington during early December 1858, he probably lost complete track of her. So too did the world after the initial flurry of publicity in the British press when S.S. Africa docked at Liverpool in January 1859. Albert G. Browne became distracted after he returned from Utah by the demands of the New England lecture circuit, attempts to build a law practice, immersion in the American Civil War, marriage to a former abolitionist, and successful adoption of the persona of a New York newspaper editor and political commentator. As a result, in 1877 Browne had to fall back on his imagination to fabricate the ending for Henrietta's story. What he wrote, then, was truly a novella not a history. He had already done that in 1859 with "The Utah Expedition: Its Causes and Consequences."

Truman Capote, take note.

TWELVE YEARS PASSED BEFORE I AGAIN SAW SALT Lake City, this time as a passenger, with my wife, on the Pacific railroad, the next summer after the silver spike was driven at Ogden.[1] Twelve years full of wonderful changes! Over the wastes which I plodded in my dreary journey with the dispatches, villages had sprung up at every railroad station. The day for such adventures as those of 1858 was past forever.

Many of my old acquaintances had been swept away in the whirlwind of the civil war. The general fell at the head of the rebel army in its hour of victory at Shiloh. The marshal, a West Virginian, fighting I do not know on which side, was killed in the Wilderness. The judge died in bed at home, the second year of

---

1   The completion ceremony for the transcontinental railroad took place not at Ogden but northwest of there at Promontory Summit, Utah Territory, on May 10, 1869. Six special metal spikes were driven into the last tie of the railroad as part of the ceremony: three golden spikes from California, one silver spike from Nevada, one iron spike with silver and gold plating from Arizona, and one regular iron spike. http://www.steamlocomotive.com/promontory/.

the war; and I was sorry to hear that he died a "copperhead."[2] Even if it was so, I am sure that the old man was honest according to his light. The attorney was living in Montana, grown rich by mining speculations, and was a candidate for Congress.

Dotson's house had disappeared with the growth of Salt Lake City. So had the garden where the Baxters hoed and sang. But Elder Josiah's cottage still was standing, with the veranda, though its western view was cut off by a row of prosperous shops. After visiting this, we mounted the hill to see if any trace was left of Elder Peckham's house. He had long been gathered to the patriarchs whose example he copied so literally.[3] There it stood, but with another polygamous tenant: a long one-story building with a dozen doors and twice as many windows,—each door opening into the former quarters of one of Peckham's wives. As we loitered in the yard, a young couple turned the corner of the building, sight-seers like ourselves; they were a square-shouldered, ruddy-faced Englishman, and his young wife, who were stopping at the same tavern with us. He was an officer of the British civil service in New Zealand, who had come up from Panama on a recent steamer and was on his way to England. We had met them first a week before, at the little inn on the shore of Lake Tahoe, that enchanted sea in the bosom of the Sierras.[4] It would be beginning another story to tell how at last in this demure little lady I recognized the elfish WARD OF THE THREE GUARDIANS.

A. G. Browne, Jr.

---

2   See Epilogue for Eckels' post-Utah fate as well as that of McCormick and Dotson.

3   Peckham's real-life counterpart, Samuel W. Richards, lived until 1909.

4   When Browne was in Utah, this body of water was known as Lake Bigler. When he published Ward, the name was transitioning to Lake Tahoe, a label the California State Legislature did not adopt officially until 1945.

GENERAL VIEW OF SALT LAKE CITY, UTAH TERRITORY.

HENRIETTA POLYDORE'S SALT LAKE CITY, 1858

A dramatic view overlooking the city, probably by a New York artist who had never seen the city. *From* Harper's Weekly, *May 15, 1858. Public domain.*

PART THREE

Meaning

Mr. H. F. Polydore, a much-respected English solicitor, desires to express his thanks all round, for the rescue of his young daughter from the sink of Mormonism . . . As the incidents which preceded the child's abduction, and captivity in Utah, have been extensively published, and as her restoration to her father is a pleasing episode of warlike operations, I suggest the propriety of letting Mr. Polydore's gratitude find vent through the [Washington] *Intelligencer* and *Union*.

U.S. AMBASSADOR GEORGE MIFFLIN DALLAS (LONDON)
TO SECRETARY OF STATE LEWIS CASS,
DECEMBER 31, 1858

Editors' Epilogue

WHAT WAS THE POST-WAR FATE OF HENRIetta Polydore, her extended family, the three so-called "guardians," and Judge Delana R. Eckels? For that matter, how did the public receive Albert G. Browne's account of all this when *Ward* appeared in *The Atlantic Monthly* twenty years later? In his closing paragraphs, Browne offered some explanations, but they were incomplete. They were also the familiar, challenging mixture of fact and fiction found throughout *Ward*.

🌿 HENRIETTA POLYDORE

Henrietta arrived in Liverpool aboard the Cunard Line's mail packet S.S. *Africa* in early January 1859, and was reunited with her father to the accompaniment of British press coverage that simply took notice of her repatriation and the legal maneuvers that accomplished it. The U.S. minister to Great Britain, George Mifflin Dallas, summarized the resolution of the affair to Secretary of State Cass, as shown in the epigraph on the preceding page. After this very brief period of excitement, Henrietta Polydore drifted into a life of anonymity and ill health in Gloucestershire with Henry Polydore. Regrettably, there were no interviews

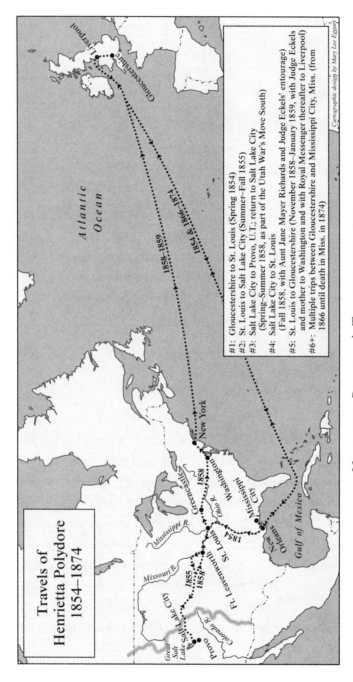

Travels of
Henrietta Polydore
1854–1874

Atlantic
Ocean

Liverpool

Gloucestershire

1858–1859

1854 & 1859–1874

New York

Washington

Greencastle

1858

Mississippi
City

Ohio R.

Mississippi R.

St. Louis

Ft. Leavenworth

1854

New
Orleans

Gulf of Mexico

1855

1858

Missouri R.

Great
Salt
Lake
Salt Lake City

Provo

Colorado R.

#1: Gloucestershire to St. Louis (Spring 1854)
#2: St. Louis to Salt Lake City (Summer–Fall 1855)
#3: Salt Lake City to Provo, U.T.; return to Salt Lake City
    (Spring–Summer 1858, as part of the Utah War's Move South)
#4: Salt Lake City to St. Louis
    (Fall 1858, with Aunt Jane Mayer Richards and Judge Eckels' entourage)
#5: St. Louis to Gloucestershire (November 1858–January 1859, with Judge Eckels
    and mother to Washington and with Royal Messenger thereafter to Liverpool)
#6+: Multiple trips between Gloucestershire and Mississippi City, Miss. (from
    1866 until death in Miss. in 1874)

Cartographic design by Mary Lee Eggart

HENRIETTA POLYDORE'S TRAVELS, 1854–1874

Map commissioned by authors; cartographer Mary Lee Eggart, Baton Rouge.

with her or follow-up stories to probe her reactions to Mormonism and the American West.[1]

Christina Rossetti was also overjoyed at the news of her cousin's return to England and soon after her arrival, perhaps before even seeing her, she composed a commemorative poem. Whether Henrietta or the rest of the family were aware of this honor is questionable, since the poem—simply titled "For H. P."—remained in holograph form among Christina's personal papers until her brother, William, found and published it posthumously in 1896:

> For H[enrietta] P[olydore]
> On the land and on the sea
> Jesus keep both you and me:
> Going out and coming in,
> Christ keep us both from shame and sin:
> In this world, in the world to come,
> Keep us safe and lead us home:
> To-day in toil, to-night in rest,
> Be best beloved and love us best.[2]

On the other hand, the extensive publicity generated by Henrietta's "case" during 1858 generated hope among other parents (and their lawyers) anxious to retrieve their own daughters from Mormonism as Henry Polydore had done. If he had succeeded by the ingenious, long-distance tactic of seeking a writ of *habeas corpus* in a U.S. district court, others would too, including one family

---

1   George Mifflin Dallas (London) to Lewis Cass (Washington), December 31, 1858, Dispatch No. 235, George Mifflin Dallas and Julia Dallas, eds., *A Series of Letters from London Written During the Years 1856, '57, '58, '59*, 2 vols. in one (Philadelphia: J. B. Lippincott & Co., 1869) 2: 75–76.

2   Christina G. Rossetti, "For H. P.," January 16, 1859, in William Michael Rossetti, ed., *New Poems by Christina Rossetti, Hitherto Unpublished or Uncollected* (New York and London: MacMillan and Co., 1896), 242 and 390.

THE CUNARD STEAM-SHIP "AFRICA."

S.S. *Africa*
The Cunard liner aboard which Henrietta Polydore sailed
from New York to Liverpool, December 1858.
Image from Harper's Weekly, March 30, 1889, public domain.

in Denmark. This is not the place for an analysis of these Poly-
dore-inspired lawsuits except to say that on the facts they were
quite different than Henrietta's case; their disposition in favor
of the defendants dampened any boomlet that might otherwise
have developed among the litigious.[3]

In some way, upon returning to England, Henrietta resumed
her formal education. While resident in Samuel W. Richards'
home as "Lucy" during the late 1850s, Richards had hoped that
she would be going to school in Salt Lake City. Whether that

---

3   Unattributed [Browne], "Interesting from Utah," Dispatch, September 10, 1858,
      New-York Tribune, October 13, 1858; "Later from Utah," Dispatch, September 15,
      1858, *New-York Tribune*, October 16, 1858.

happened is unknown, but the English census of 1861 lists her as among the "scholars" at a private school in County Surrey. Since her father was still working in Gloucestershire, it is likely that this was a boarding school, perhaps of the type in which her parents had enrolled her in Lincolnshire during the early 1850s.[4]

Religiously, Henrietta never converted to Mormonism, although, as discussed below, in 1897 her mother performed Latter-day Saint rites on her behalf vicariously in the Salt Lake Temple. From Christina Rossetti's 1866 correspondence, it is clear that, notwithstanding the conversion of her mother and Mayer relatives, young Henrietta remained an observant Roman Catholic.[5]

By 1864, if not earlier, it was also evident that Henrietta had contracted tuberculosis or "consumption" as it was then called. Precisely how and when she became infected is unknown, although during the twentieth century an article in a publication of the Daughters of Utah Pioneers asserted that she became tubercular in England without clarifying whether this occurred before she left for America in 1854 or after her return in 1859.[6] Jane Mayer Richards also had the disease in the 1860s. Another of the unknowns is whether Jane's infection derived from Henrietta's (or vice versa), or whether the two cases were independent of one another and therefore coincidental.

What is clear is that beginning in the 1860s young Henrietta's life and identity were defined *de facto* by her affliction. Virtually no letter among the Rossetti family's voluminous correspondence

4   England and Wales Census, 1861, Kingston, County Surrey.
5   Christina G. Rossetti to Anne Burrows Gilchrist, May 1866, Harrison, ed., *The Letters of Christina Rossetti*, 1:270–71.
6   Kate B. Carter, comp., "Historic Letters," in Daughters of Utah Pioneers, *Lesson for March 1969*, 396. Carter's undocumented assertion about Henrietta's infection probably came from Latter-day Saint descendants of her mother's Mayer family resident in Utah after moving from the South near the turn of the twentieth century.

for the period mentions Henrietta without referring to her illness. For example, while visiting the Polydores in Gloucester during the summer of 1867, Christina Rossetti wrote a friend:

> First for my one bit of good news: Henrietta's attack that we vaguely heard of appears not to have been very marked or novel; and *now* she seems to me tolerably well in health, though I should like to see her freer from weariness and languor and with more bloom on her cheeks. However we trot bravely about this pretty country and find small topics of conversation and are very quiet and friendly. Whether we shall have her in Euston Square [London] before the summer is over I don't know; she seems of opinion that her Father must not be abandoned to [servant] Bridget's cookery, and that her own finger is needed in the pie: but I hope she will come after all.[7]

It also became obvious that, as Henrietta grew older and the post–Civil War American South became more stable, she was determined to visit her mother and Mayer relatives, all of whom had remained in the South after abandoning their original plans to emigrate to Utah Territory in 1857. Accordingly, with the apparent consent and financial support of her estranged parents, Henrietta crossed the Atlantic several times, accompanied by a long-time companion-attendant identified only as an American named "Marianne." Saddened by this complex family scene and a major deterioration in Henrietta's health once back in the United States, Christina wrote in 1869:

> My main news is sad: a letter from Henrietta gives a depressing account of her health which rendered her, at the time of writing, altogether unfit to start on her homeward voyage. Her poor father is disappointed keenly as you may think, though heartily

<hr>

7   Christina G. Rossetti to Amelia Barnard Heimann, July 17, 1867, Harrison, ed., *The Letters of Christina Rossetti*, 1:299.

acquiescent in the necessity for his disappointment. Now I can form no opinion at all as to when she may be expected in England, if indeed it is not too bold even to speak so confidently of her ultimate return. How terribly, in divided homes and interests, and some times in hearts torn asunder, do children pay the penalty of their parents' mistakes.[8]

Finally, on September 30, 1874, after several more Atlantic crossings and a stay of more than a year with her mother and the Mayers, Henrietta died at Mississippi City on the Gulf of Mexico at age twenty-eight. In England there had been premonitions that the end was near; in June 1874 Christina Rossetti wrote her painter-brother, Dante, "Uncle Henry [Polydore] returns to Gloucester today, after a 3 weeks visit to my Aunts in [London's] Bloomsbury Square. Naturally enough he is saddened and uneasy on his poor Henrietta's account, all the news of her being grave if not alarming." Once word of her passing reached London, Christina wrote a friend, "Our poor Henrietta is I hope the gainer by this change, which yet is so awful to flesh & blood; but her poor parents who remain behind are indeed to be pitied."[9]

Henrietta had never returned to Utah, and there is no record that she communicated with Albert G. Browne, Jr. after presumably seeing him in Washington during December 1858. At her death, Henrietta was, of course, unaware that Albert would publish *Ward* three years later. As discussed earlier, there were multiple reasons why Browne wrote as he did in 1877, but if he knew Henrietta had died in 1874, her passing may have removed inhibitions while serving as a catalyst for his resolve to tell her story.

---

8   Christina G. Rossetti to Amelia Barnard Heimann, May 24, 1869, ibid, 323.

9   Christina G. Rossetti to Dante Gabriel Rossetti, June 22, 1874, and to Amelia Barnard Heimann, October 20, 1874, both ibid, 2: 17 and 28.

☙ The Polydore-Richards-Rossetti Extended Family

In November 1858, Jane Mayer Richards and infant son Phineas, Henrietta Polydore, Elizabeth Cotton, Mary Tecumbiats, and Judge Eckels debarked from a Missouri River packet at St. Louis with plans to continue east by rail. In St. Louis, the party was confronted by Henrietta's mother, who had ascended the Mississippi from the Polydore-Mayer family's cotton farm in Hillsboro, Union County, Arkansas, the haven to which they had moved from New Orleans when it became clear that the Utah War would disrupt their plans to move west via the overland trail. Whether Judge Eckels had been alerted to this rendezvous by Jane Richards is unclear, but it soon was evident that Mrs. Polydore was determined to dissuade him from taking her daughter farther east for repatriation. At bare minimum she intended to accompany him first to his home in Greencastle, Indiana (to drop Elizabeth and Mary), and then to Washington with young Henrietta to carry her campaign to the British Legation. As the judge's eclectic entourage moved east, Jane and Phineas Richards remained in St. Louis to await her sister's return from the Atlantic Coast so that they might then together steam down the Mississippi to Arkansas.

Attuned to the family and legal drama involved in what was unfolding in St. Louis and titillated by Judge Eckels' fabrication of a 500-mile pursuit across the plains by Mormon Danites, the national press rose to the opportunity. In the process, the newspapers generated a plethora of confusing stories about who was traveling with whom and for what purpose. The clearest record we have of what transpired immediately before Henrietta steamed for England on December 8 was created by E. M. Archbold, the harried British consul in New York, for the Earl of Malmesbury, the British foreign secretary in London:

HENRIETTA POLYDORE'S ANGLO-ITALIAN ROSSETTI COUSINS
left to right   Painter Dante Gabriel, poet Christina Georgina, mother Frances
Mary, and writer William Michael. Photo (London 1863) by Oxford University
mathematician and famous novelist "Lewis Carroll." *Courtesy Alamy Photos.*

I have the honor to report to your Lordship that Miss Polydore
who arrived at Washington from Utah in charge of Judge Eckels
a few days since has been forwarded to my care from Washington by Lord Napier in charge of the Messenger of the Legation
and reached my house about four o'clock this morning. I had
secured her passage from hence to Liverpool by the Royal Mail
S.S. *Africa* which sails at the unusually early [hour] of half past
nine, this morning, and I am now about to proceed to the ship

at Jersey City to place Miss P. in charge of Captain Shannon whom I have instructed immediately on his reaching Liverpool to telegraph Mr. Polydore of his daughter's arrival. Mrs. Polydore attached herself to her daughter at St. Louis accompanying her to Washington from where they were both inmates of Lord Napier's house. She has likewise accompanied her child to New York and is now with her in my house; and although tremendously opposed to her daughter's return to England will hardly have time if she contemplates such a proceeding to take any legal steps to delay Miss Polydore's departure.[10]

⚜ JANE MAYER RICHARDS

Once the extended Polydore-Mayer family (minus young Henrietta) regrouped in Arkansas in early January 1859, Jane set about enjoying the company of her parents and siblings, whom she had not seen for nearly five years, while introducing them to infant Phineas H. Richards, soon called "Henry." From available information, the year passed pleasantly for this group until a letter arrived from Judge Eckels (then back in Utah) informing Jane that Samuel had taken a sixth wife. It is not known precisely what Eckels wrote Jane about this sealing, but it had taken place on January 27, 1859, four months after she left Salt Lake City, and involved thirty-year-old Elizabeth Whitaker Cain, widow of Samuel's business partner and their neighbor. Oddly, on the day of his sealing to Mrs. Cain, Samuel wrote a long newsy letter to Jane that included comments about each of his other wives but no reference to the sixth and newest one. Upset that she had not

---

10   E.M. Archbold to Lord Malmesbury, December 8, 1858, Dispatch No. 53, F.O. 282/5, Records of the Foreign Office, British National Archives, Kew. This dispatch traveled with Henrietta aboard S.S. *Africa* and would have been couriered to the foreign office immediately upon arrival in Liverpool.

heard this news directly from her husband, Jane said so, receiving in response an explanation from Samuel that he had not wanted to entrust such sensitive information to a letter out of fear of mail interception and possible publication. With plural marriage a publicly acknowledged practice of the Latter-day Saints since 1852, and with Brigham Young having granted an interview to Horace Greeley of the *New-York Tribune* during the summer of 1859, such an explanation seems disingenuous.

Adding to the insensitivity of it all, on August 18, 1859, Samuel wrote Jane to list the names of his wives and again chose not to mention Elizabeth: "Mary, Mary Ann, Helena, Mary Amelia, and all send love to you. What a row of names, one can write when they begin." In 1865, after Jane had returned to Salt Lake City, Henrietta Mayer Polydore unwittingly added to the potential complexity of the family marital arrangements by writing to her sister, "I do not see how a little man like our good brother Samuel does with such a tribe about him but his case is hopeless. Give my best love to him if he feels like taking another wife and that as old . . . as myself, send me word immediately. . . . Has Mr. [Brigham] Young got all the wives he wants yet perhaps I may get a chance there yet."[11]

---

11   For reasons that are unclear, the Church History Library has closed access to its collection containing the letters sent by Jane Mayer Richards during 1859, although many of Samuel W. Richards' are available. Accordingly, our account of the Jane-Samuel communications about his 1859 marriage is based on notes taken about this material in 2002 when this collection was open to researchers. Ardis E. Parshall to MacKinnon, email, November 14, 2002, copy in MacKinnon's research files. See also Maurine Carr Ward, "Samuel Whitney Richards, His Wives, Children, and Descendants," internet essay, http://www.n1.net/~mcward/swr.htm, accessed August 4, 2002; and Samuel W. Richards (Salt Lake City) to Jane Mayer Richards (Arkansas), January 27 and August 18, 1859, Samuel W. Richards Papers as well as Henrietta Mayer Polydore (Monroe, La.) to Jane Mayer Richards (Salt Lake City), November 20, 1865, Jane Mayer Richards Correspondence, all Church History Library.

In *Ward* A. G. Browne wrote that Jane Mayer Richards had approached Judge Eckels about escorting Henrietta Polydore east in order to escape Mormonism. There is no reason to accept that speculation; she appears to have been a committed Latter-day Saint for the rest of her life and, notwithstanding her husband's insensitivity in communications, gave every sign of wanting to return to her communal home in Salt Lake City. In January 1859 Samuel W. Richards began planning for a return to take place at a seemingly open-ended time: "Please inform me what will be your pleasure as to the time and manner of conveyance upon your return home. This will I presume depend some upon how many of your friends [family] come with you."[12]

Because of the inaccessibility of Jane's correspondence, it is difficult to determine what then happened and why. What is known is that Jane and Phineas did not cross the plains in 1859 or 1860, and her son died of unknown cause at age four in 1861, presumably in Arkansas, where his grandfather Mayer died in 1864. Jane did not return to Utah until 1865 because of the war-time closure of the Mississippi River to civilian traffic and similar disruptions to Mormon use of the overland trail.[13] On May 15, 1867, Jane

---

12 Samuel W. Richards (Salt Lake City) to Jane Mayer Richards (Arkansas), January 27, 1859, Samuel W. Richards papers, ibid.

13 For a glimpse of the difficulty of civilian travel on the Mississippi River before the fall of Vicksburg in July 1863, see Sophia ("Sophy") Mayer (New Orleans) to Samuel W. Richards (Salt Lake City), March 7, 1863: "I hope you will write [wife] Jane a long letter—I am going to try every means of getting there [Arkansas]. If I can go [upriver] on a Gunboat I would with pleasure. I feel as tho I don't care for shot or shell, so long as I could see them again—but if I cannot go I may have another opportunity of sending [mail] to Jane. I know how bad she feels at home [on the Mayer farm] unable to hear from you so write soon without any delay to me & I will forward to her." Jane Mayer Richards, Correspondence 1857–1867, MS 3528, Church History Library. Transcontinental stagecoach travel between St. Louis and California via the Overland Mail Company was prohibitively expensive ($200) and was discontinued in March 1861 because of the likelihood of war.

died in Salt Lake City, a victim of the tuberculosis that would claim Henrietta seven years later and that had perhaps taken her only child six years earlier. She was buried in the Richards family plot along with her five sister wives, all of whom had been born in England.

Although Jane Mayer Richards was not a longtime resident of Salt Lake City, she was well-received in the city's influential Fourteenth Ward and its Women's Relief Society. This acceptance must have contributed to young Henrietta's sense of wellbeing in the Richards household during her "Lucy" years and perhaps accounted for her initial resistance to her court-ordered repatriation to England. Upon Jane's death, Eliza Roxcy Snow composed a memorial poem, a high honor from Mormonism's poet laureate who was also a wife of Brigham Young and widow of Joseph Smith. (See Appendix B.) One of the most moving tributes to Jane was a long letter of condolence written by one of her close friends to Samuel in 1867. Enigmatically, this letter closed with the thought, "There is one thing I am glad about that is that dear Jane lived to know that her husband loved her."[14]

❦ HENRIETTA MAYER POLYDORE

As Jane rose in the esteem of her neighbors after the Civil War, the members of her extended Mayer family prospered in the American South, even during the agony of Reconstruction. In 1866 the family obtained a long-term lease on the Barnes Hotel, a large, upscale resort on the Gulf Coast in Mississippi's Harrison County near what is now Gulfport. As the family left rural Arkansas behind, the titular leader of the Barnes Hotel venture

---

14   Mrs. M. Morrison to Samuel W. Richards, May 26, 1867, Kate B. Carter, ed., "Historic Letters," 397.

was Henrietta Mayer Polydore's brother, John D. Mayer, but one senses that she, not he, was the catalyst for this enterprise's success.[15] After all, it was Henrietta who had moved the entire family across the Atlantic in 1856 to New Orleans while penniless and deathly ill; she was the one who bearded Judge Eckels, Lord Napier, and Consul Archbold in St. Louis, Washington, and Manhattan in pursuit of her daughter's well-being. It was to Mississippi City and the Barnes Hotel that young Henrietta episodically crossed the Atlantic seeking respite from the ravages of consumption; it was there, in her mother's care, she died in 1874, hard in the lee of President Jefferson Davis' neighboring plantation-in-exile, "Beauvoir." It was also to mother Henrietta's care that Dante Gabriel Rossetti later commended his mistress-model, Fanny Cornforth. Beset by illness and contemplating his own mortality, Dante instructed brother William that upon his death he was to send "a letter for Mrs. Polydore, a relation who had joined the Latter-day Saints in Utah, asking for 'exile' for Fanny, as it was felt that this would be a better prospect than her remaining in England." Henrietta's family reciprocated this confidence in naming her youngest niece Christina Rossetti Mayer.[16]

---

15   For a description of the Barnes Hotel and the family's plans for operating it, see Henrietta Mayer Polydore (Monroe, La.) to Jane Mayer Richards (Salt Lake City), November 20, 1865, Jane Mayer Richards Correspondence, Church History Library. The text of this letter is also available in Kate B. Carter, comp., "Historic Letters," 393–95. The phrasing of this letter makes clear that Jane returned to Utah in 1865. The 1866 legal arrangement to acquire the hotel from William Barnes seems to have been a lease with an option to buy for $25,000, a substantial sum for that time. This amount would be consistent with John D. Mayer's listing in the 1870 U.S. Census for Harrison County as the possessor of $30,000 in real property and $5,500 in personal property.

16   Kirsty Stonell Walker, *Stunner: The Fall and Rise of Fanny Cornforth* (Lulu.com, 2006), 54n12.

In the late 1880s the Polydore-Mayer family lost control of the Barnes, with some members then emigrating to Utah while others gravitated to Louisiana. In 1905, with typical enterprise, Henrietta won appointment as postmistress in St. Helena Parish, Louisiana, but soon relocated to Utah to live with a brother, first in Ogden and then Pleasant Grove. In the latter town she died at age eighty-nine on April 11, 1911, noticed only in a *Deseret News* obituary riddled with inaccuracies and devoid of any reference to her briefly famous daughter.[17] She was the last to go of the people directly associated with the story Albert Browne had presented as a non-fiction novel thirty-four years earlier.

Before dying, Henrietta Mayer Polydore trekked to the new Salt Lake Temple and there performed several of Mormonism's most sacred rites for the posthumous benefit of her Roman Catholic daughter: baptism and the endowment ritual. In 2004, in another temple, some unknown Latter-day Saint performed a rite by which Henrietta became sealed for all eternity to both her parents, notwithstanding their estrangement in life.[18] It was an ending to young Henrietta's story far different than the fate in colonial New Zealand to which Browne consigned her in concluding *The Ward of the Three Guardians*.

---

17   *City Directory, Ogden, Weber County, Utah, 1911*; "Recent Deaths," *Deseret Evening News*, April 13, 1911, 8/5–6.

18   Henrietta Polydore records accessed via FamilySearch.org and research notes, Ardis E. Parshall to MacKinnon, email of August 23, 2020. Since this temple work was performed in Salt Lake City by Henrietta's mother during August 1897, it is likely she traveled from Louisiana on a visit via the transcontinental railroad before relocating permanently to Ogden.

⚜ SAMUEL W. RICHARDS

After Jane's return to Samuel Richards' home from Arkansas in 1865, his life settled into a less dramatic routine in which he worked in a variety of enterprises to support his family (six wives and nineteen children) and served his church. There were no more marriages or international missions, although in the 1890s he was called to preside over the Latter-day Saints' Eastern States Mission in New York. In his church, Samuel never rose to become an apostle, or "face card" as Albert Browne's fictive Jim Bridger in *Ward* dubbed the members of The Quorum of the Twelve. He served for several years in Utah Territory's Legislative Assembly and in multiple municipal/county offices; during Utah's Black Hawk War of 1865–67, he was a Nauvoo Legion colonel.[19]

From the distance of the twenty-first century, it is easy to conclude that Samuel W. Richards' two assignments to preside over the British Mission during the 1850s were the high point of his life. Thereafter, he did not continue to rise to a level of responsibility in the commercial, ecclesiastical, or military realms that matched the accomplishments of his brother, Franklin D. Richards, or their uncle, Willard D. Richards, who was Brigham Young's longtime second counselor in The First Presidency. To say that Samuel failed to fulfill his potential is too judgmental, but there were occasional telltales in the wind signaling shortfalls, as men of lesser sophistication, physical attractiveness, and family connections inexplicably passed him by. Perhaps emblematic of the problem was the decline in Richards' standing with Brigham Young during the Utah War.

In February 1856 President Young had officiated at the ceremony

---

19 Andrew Jenson, *Latter-day Saint Biographical* Dictionary, 4 vols. (Salt Lake City: Deseret News Press, 1901–1936), 1:718–19 and 4:318.

by which Samuel had taken Jane Mayer as his fourth wife, with
Henrietta Polydore or "Lucy" in tow. Eighteen months later, as
the Utah War began, Young selected Richards to lead the British
Mission again—this time when Latter-day Saint morale in Great
Britain needed invigoration and emigration to the United States
had to be curtailed or redirected to Canada. At the same time,
Young entrusted Samuel with two other collateral but important
assignments to be accomplished en route from Salt Lake City to
Liverpool: gathering military intelligence about the Utah Expedition as he encountered it on the overland trail; and briefing
Thomas L. Kane on Young's plans for the defense of Utah. The
latter involved potentially treasonous information Young was
unwilling to commit to writing let alone transmit by mail.

The first of these tasks Richards performed well, sending
Young a steady flow of detailed reports on troop movements from
the trail, Forts Laramie, Kearny, and Leavenworth, and the decks
of Missouri River steamboats. But when Samuel reached Philadelphia in mid-September 1857, his judgment faltered. There, he
found Kane had withdrawn from the city, frustrated over President Buchanan's unwillingness to accept his advice on Latter-day
Saint affairs; he was spending the summer not in Philadelphia
but in the mountains of western Pennsylvania. Instead of changing his plans and traveling a few hundred miles more to meet
with Kane in person, Richards kept to his original itinerary,
moved on from Philadelphia to New York and Boston, and took
ship for Liverpool. In Kane's Independence Hall office Samuel
left an opaquely worded message noting the insecurity of written communications and promising to share Brigham Young's
thoughts in full at some future date when he would again revisit
Philadelphia while returning from England. Kane did not see
this note until weeks later, and even then its phrasing left him

uninformed about Young's war strategy. There is no record of
Brigham Young's reaction to this chain of events, but it is unlikely
that he was pleased with Richards' lack of urgency, inflexibility,
and unwillingness to improvise.[20]

The next strain on the Young-Richards relationship came
in January 1858 with the arrival in Salt Lake City of Apostles
Ezra T. Benson and Orson Pratt, Richards' predecessors as leaders of the British Mission. They carried to Salt Lake City with
them the mission's financial records for their period of stewardship and also for the years of Samuel Richards' first assignment
there (1851–54), ledgers that President Young the micro-manager
subjected to greater scrutiny than one might typically expect
from a senior leader. The records revealed signs of an undesirable
laxness at the British Mission in handling tithing funds. Some
inflows from members went uncredited (unrecorded), and there
was undocumented, perhaps excessive, use of such funds to cover
travel and other out-of-pocket expenses incurred by leaders at the
regional organizations in England, Scotland, and Wales, if not
the mission's headquarters in Liverpool. On March 5, 1858, a time
when Brigham Young was engaged in a critical phase of the Utah
War, he took time to send a confidential letter to Asa S. Calkin,
Richards' counselor in Liverpool and his successor-designate: "Be

20   Brigham Young, Heber C. Kimball, and Daniel H. Wells to Samuel W. Richards
and George Snider, August 5, 1857, C R 1234/1, Box 3, Letterpress Copybook, vol. 3,
781–85, and Richards to Young, September 19, 1857, both Brigham Young Collection, Church History Library; MacKinnon, ed., At Sword's Point, Part 1, 252–56,
406–409. Because of the example he set with his own obsession about mail monitoring by federal postmasters, Young suffered several such communications gaps
during key junctures in the Utah War such as during the winter of 1858 when congressional delegate John M. Bernhisel declined to inform Young by mail that he and
Walter Murray Gibson were discussing with President Buchanan the possibility of
a Latter-day Saint mass exodus to an island in the Dutch East Indies in exchange
for a U.S. government buy-out of properties in Utah. At Sword's Point, Part 2, 394.

sure, on the first opportunity to inform me precisely how much Tithing funds Brother Samuel W. Richards drew from the Liverpool Office, or from any other source, during his late sojourn in England: also, specify the amount of *each kind* of such funds drawn by brother Samuel, if in any kind but coin. Be pleased to make no mention of this matter as such information I needed at this office or the current transaction of business, and is a matter which would benefit no one by being noised abroad." Without waiting for Calkin's report, Young rewarded him with a gratuitous authorization to take another wife on an open-ended basis.[21]

It is unclear what repercussions, if any, awaited Samuel when he returned to Utah in mid-May 1858 and reported to Brigham Young during the Move South after evading the army near Forts Laramie and Bridger. At about this time, though, Young decided to shut down a publishing venture that Richards had earlier begun in Liverpool with Orson Pratt on a speculative, personal business. It was a decision that cost Samuel thousands of dollars, and, although he accepted its ruinous financial consequences at the time, as soon as Young died in 1877 he put out feelers seeking reimbursement. Samuel Richards' description to Pratt of what had happened spoke volumes about his relationship with Brigham Young by the end of the Utah War:

---

21 Brigham Young to Asa S. Calkin, February 4 and March 5, 1858, both in Calkin Journal, April 20 and May 25, 1858, MS 8138, Church History Library. In thinking about Brigham Young's administrative style in a different context, one of this volume's editors wrote: "In addition to his plethora of formal church, civil, and military titles, Brigham Young was an accomplished woodworker, glazer, and painter as well as an amateur architect and civil engineer. For purposes of this essay, I will argue that, in many respects, Young was also at heart an auditor, although he would probably bridle at such a descriptor." MacKinnon, "Off-the-Books Warfare: Financing the Utah War's Standing Army of Israel," in Matthew C. Godfrey and Michael Hubbard MacKay, eds., *Business and Religion: The Intersection of Faith and Finance* (Provo and Salt Lake City: BYU Religious Studies Center and Deseret Book Co., 2019), 177.

I trust no apology will be needed for the liberty I take in requesting your consideration of the following facts which a severe
pres[s]ure of unfavorable pecuniary circumstances induce me to
state. . . . The late action of Prest. Young and others through his
influence, has served to so embarrass me in circumstances that
I am unable to suitably provide for the wants of a large family
now looking to me for the necessaries of life, & social advantages.
This compels me to inquire where I may with propriety apply for
such favors as might aid me in my necessities, and do no injus-
tice to others. . . . I came home from that long and arduous Mission [in 1854] almost without means, without horses, stock, or
even money enough to finish off a small house I had commenced
before leaving [for England], and found myself in debt. . . . I have
no inclination to inquire here where the responsibility of the loss
in that transaction would rest if I had made the demand upon
Prest. Young. . . . While Prest. Young was with us [alive] I did not
wish to call up any thing that would aggravate feelings relating to
the past, and upon which he seemed very sensitive.[22]

Perhaps sensing that he had fallen out of Brigham Young's good
graces, Samuel W. Richards waited four days after Judge Eckels'
adjudication of the Polydore case and then proffered Young a gift
calculated to catch his interest—instructions for use of an arcane
code he had brought home from England that spring. At first
blush this gift might not seem like the stuff with which to ingra-
tiate oneself with a religious leader, but Richards knew first-hand
of Young's anxiety about interception of his correspondence and
the lengths to which he went to avoid use of the U.S. mails while
himself monitoring, if not intercepting, the letters of non-Mormons passing through Salt Lake City's post office. Pandering to

---

22   Samuel W. Richards to Orson Pratt, November 16, 1878, Samuel W. Richards
      Papers, Church History Library. Whatever financial pressures beset Richards
      during the mid-1850s, they did not preclude his third, fourth, and fifth marriages
      and all the responsibilities that went with them during 1855–56.

this near-obsession with mail security and intelligence gathering, Richards provided his leader with "a complete system by which secret correspondence can be maintained in time of war, or whenever such correspondence is advisable. It was arranged by Elder Wm. Budge in England, who, with only one or two others, have any knowledge of the system. It is now presented to President Brigham Young for his examination and use, if approved by him. N[ota]. B[ene]. the [code] Diagram is subject to many variations should the present form of it be discovered so universally as to destroy its utility."[23]

For those wondering why Brigham Young showed no interest in the Henrietta Polydore case during its adjudication in August 1858, the answer may lay with the distractions of his own legal and emotional problems, or, alternatively, with Young's view of the family which had sequestered "Lucy" since 1855. Samuel W. Richards died in Salt Lake City in November 1909 at age eighty-five, survived by only one of his many wives, the former Mary Ann Parker (his second). Richards was a respected senior leader of his community with a wide variety of experiences, but not one of Jim Bridger's "face cards" or Brigham Young's apostles.

⚜ CHRISTINA AND DANTE ROSSETTI

Life ended poorly for Henrietta's cousins, Dante and Christina Rossetti. Known primarily as a painter, Dante also tried his hand at poetry without much success. Many of his paintings were of his wife (Elizabeth Siddal), his mistress (Fanny Cornforth), and the wife of one of his close friends (Jane Morris). Following his wife's

---

23 Richards to Young, August 9, 1858, Collection MS 4775, Church History Library. The editors thank Utah historian Ardis E. Parshall for access to this document as well as her encyclopedic knowledge of the codes and ciphers used by Latter-day Saint leaders during the nineteenth century.

death in 1862, possibly a suicide from an overdose of laudanum, he buried many of his poems with her (but later dug them up and published them). He suffered from depression, drug addiction, and Bright's Disease (a kidney disease that eventually paralyzed him). He died on Easter Sunday in 1882.[24]

While Henrietta was traveling with her three guardians, her cousin Christina was experiencing a personal religious crisis in England during which time "she wrote several of her most heart-felt poems." She rejected three serious suitors through the years and never married. Generally considered in delicate and ill health throughout her life, she was diagnosed with Graves Disease in the early 1870s, which tormented her for the rest of her life. She continued to write and publish poetry until shortly before her death on December 29, 1894.[25]

⚜ ALBERT G. BROWNE, JR.

Browne, of course, is largely absent from his own tale except for the role of narrator and as a courier crossing the plains during the winter of 1858. We also see him fleetingly in Salt Lake City during the summer of 1870 at the novella's conclusion, a wholly fictive ending. What became of him?

In early October 1858, three months after the Utah Expedition marched into Salt Lake City and more than a year after he left home, A. G. Browne began to think about leaving Utah. With the departure of Judge Eckels and completion of the U.S. district court's summer term, his meager legal practice atrophied further. He finished his $200-per-month engagement for the *New-York Tribune* with an October 8 dispatch describing the "new" Camp

24   See Joseph Knight, *Life of Dante Gabriel Rossetti* (London: Walter Scott, 1887).
25   Lindsay Duguid: "Rossetti, Christina Georgina (1830–1894)," *Oxford Dictionary of National Biography* (Oxford: Oxford University Press, 2009).

Floyd. Browne knew from hard experience that if he did not start east soon, winter weather would trap him in Utah until spring. On October 15 he departed Salt Lake City in clear weather, presumably aboard the Hockaday Mail. That night a storm deposited three to four inches of snow in town while creating drifts three feet deep on Big Mountain in the Wasatch Range.[26]

Albert arrived in Salem just in time for Thanksgiving much to the relief of his mother, who had long feared for his life in proximity to a Latter-day Saint population she viewed through the lens of New England Protestantism's most extreme stereotypes.[27] On November 30 he left home again, this time to visit Washington, where, as his mother described it, "he is to restore to the British Government his young client from Utah, Miss Polydore." There too he was able to compare notes at leisure with two of his mentors, Judge Eckels and Robert Carter, then the *New-York Tribune's* capital correspondent.[28] Washington also offered Browne prospects for continued newspaper work. His mother's diary indicates he stayed in Washington for a few weeks to write for the Boston *Daily Advertiser* and, with the return of Congress for its new session, perhaps intended to remain in the capital for the winter as he had once promised Senator Charles Sumner he would do. Her observation was, "He is working hard. Launched forth upon the Ocean of Life, he now feels he *must* struggle by his own individual

---

26 For a press account of Browne's travel between Salt Lake City and St. Louis, see "Arrival of the Salt Lake Mail. Later News from Camp Floyd and Salt Lake. Snow 3 Feet deep in the Mountains," St. Louis *Democrat*, November 16, 1858, reprinted in Alton, Ill., *Weekly Courier*, November 18, 1858, 2/6.

27 Examples of Mrs. Browne's apprehensions throughout the war and in connection with her son's travel, may be found in letters to her daughter and her diary: Sarah Smith Cox Browne to Sarah Ellen ("Nellie") Browne, October 30, November 14 and 18, December 18, 1857, and May 18, 1858, and diary, September 6, 16, 21, 27 and October 16 and 24, 1858, all in Browne Family Papers, MC 298, Schlesinger Library, Radcliffe Institute.

28 Sarah Smith Cox Browne Diary, November 30, 1858.

forces." Early in the twentieth century, Browne's widow noted: "In 1859–60 resided in Washington, D.C. on law business with British Legation and correspondent Boston *Advertiser*."[29]

Whether in Washington or Massachusetts, Browne spent much of early 1859 writing about Utah. This work took the form of a lecture he later delivered at the Salem Lyceum and elsewhere in Massachusetts ("Utah and the Mormons") and then, beginning in March, his three-part essay ("The Utah Expedition: Its Causes and Consequences") appeared in *The Atlantic Monthly*.[30] While all of this work reflected an unmistakable intolerance of Mormonism, Browne muted the extremism of his private and public remarks during October–November 1857, especially his advocacy of lynch law for Brigham Young. It was a mellowing

---

29   Ibid., December 18, 1858; Martha Griffith Browne, undated holograph biographical sketch, Albert G. Browne, Jr. File, Records of the [Harvard] Class of 1853 Secretary.

30   A brief notice that Browne delivered a talk titled "Utah and the Mormons" as part of the Salem Lyceum's 1859–60 course of lectures appears in *Historical Sketch of the Salem Lyceum, With a List of the Officers and Lecturers, Since Its Formation in 1830 . . .* (Salem, Mass.: Press of the Salem Gazette, 1879), 58. Browne's papers contain a long, untitled and undated holograph manuscript dealing with Utah and Latter-day Saint affairs that formed the basis for his lectures on this subject before the Civil War and thereafter. Only a small portion of this material deals with the Utah Expedition, and of that the most relevant part is Browne's exposition of the remedy for "the Mormon problem": congressional enforcement of laws, and, lacking/failing that, expulsion or buy-out of the Latter-day Saints with an intent to motivate them to leave the United States for an unspecified Polynesian island. Browne Family Papers, MC 298, Series II (Other Papers), Box 5, Folder 130, Schlesinger Library, Radcliffe Institute.

Appearance of the first and second installments of Browne's 1859 *Atlantic Monthly* essay came in close proximity to Thomas L. Kane's delivery of his own lecture, titled "The Executive in Utah," at the New-York Historical Society on March 21, 1859. Kane's lecture was designed to thwart President Buchanan's intent to remove from office Alfred Cumming, Brigham Young's gubernatorial successor. Kane's awareness that Browne was working on a lecture and essay about Utah affairs during the winter of 1859 may have motivated him to solicit an invitation to deliver his own account of that subject in New York. See MacKinnon, "Saving the Governor's Bacon: Thomas L. Kane's Political Defense of Alfred Cumming, 1859," *Utah Historical Quarterly* 89 (Fall 2021): 323–45.

of Browne's earlier views about Latter-day Saint leaders that prompted one newspaper correspondent to comment in September 1858: "Brown[e], of the New York *Tribune*, has been apologizing to some of his Mormon acquaintance[s] for writing such strong anti-Mormon letters from Camp Scott, last winter. He says that since he arrived in the Territory and mixed with the people, he has formed quite a different opinion of the citizens."[31]

In October 1859, without mentioning either his lecture or essay, Browne wrote William A. Carter at Fort Bridger to reminisce:

> We fought through the Utah War together—the sole bloodshed in which appears to have been that of several thousands of oxen. We ate jerked beef, slept on Mackinaw blankets, lived in smoky Sibley tents, and cursed the Mormons with entire fellow-sympathy. . . . I am settled quietly in the practice of law here in Boston [with John A. Andrew], and my only hope of seeing Utah again is in some summer-excursion across the Plains. But I have not lost any interest in the welfare of all my friends of 1857 and 1858, and I often remember them—each & all—and always with regard.[32]

Four months later he wrote to Capt. John W. Phelps, the Utah Expedition's former chief of artillery, about the prospects for congressional passage of anti-polygamy legislation.[33]

---

31 "McGregor" [pseud.], Dispatch, August 13, 1858, St. Louis *Republican*, reprinted in Indianapolis *Daily State Sentinel*, September 10, 1858, 2/1.

32 Albert G. Browne, Jr. to William A. Carter, October 22, 1859, William Alexander Carter Correspondence, 1859–1872, Accn 2496, Box 1, Special Collections, University of Utah, Salt Lake City.

33 Albert G. Browne, Jr. to John W. Phelps, February 17, 1860, John Wolcott Phelps Papers, 1835–1884, MSA 611, Vermont Historical Society Library, Barre, Vt. When Browne wrote Phelps he was living in his native Vermont, to which he had returned after resigning his commission at Camp Floyd in 1859 in disgust over the Buchanan administration's Mormon policy and the absence of promotion prospects. With the Civil War Phelps became a brigadier general of volunteers, but he resigned again over the Lincoln administration's slowness to emancipate and recruit blacks into the Union Army.

In January 1861, with the Secession Crisis in mid-passage, law-yer Andrew became Massachusetts' governor. Among his first acts was appointment of Browne as his confidential secretary, and among Albert's initial duties was a clandestine mission to the governors of New Hampshire and Maine. It was a task similar to Browne's eastbound trek in the winter of 1858 to warn General Scott and the Buchanan administration of Brigham Young's plans for a spring offensive. Governor Andrew asked Browne to sensitize the governors of northern New England to the likelihood of disunion while urging them to emulate Massachusetts in putting their state militias on a war footing. When the great conflict came in April, it was not accidental that regiments from the Bay State were the first to come to Abraham Lincoln's and Washington's defense. Browne became Governor Andrew's military secretary with the rank of lieutenant colonel in the Union Army.[34]

Colonel Browne's wartime service on behalf of Massachusetts and the Union was tireless, ubiquitous, and effective, earning him the nickname "Governor No. 2."[35] Mid-way through the conflict Governor Andrew permitted Browne to travel south with the Union Army to assist his ailing father, whom President Lincoln had appointed a special Treasury agent to superintend the disposition of captured Confederate cotton. Near the end of the conflict, Andrew tasked Browne to correspond with Oregon's governor to devise a scheme by which Massachusetts war widows and spinsters might emigrate to the Pacific Coast to redress

34 William Schouler, *A History of Massachusetts in the Civil War* (Boston: E. P. Dutton & Co., 1868), 15–17; Richard F. Miller, "Brahmin Janissaries: John A. Andrew Mobilizes Massachusetts' Upper Classes for the Civil War," *The New England Quarterly* 75 (June 2002): 204–34.

35 This nickname appeared in one of the many obituaries for Browne. "Recent Deaths," Lowell, Mass. *Daily Courier*, June 27, 1891, 7/2. According to *Ward* illiterate frontiersman Jim Bridger called him "Doctor" in recognition of his Ph.D. degree from Heidelberg, and Browne's mother referred to him in her diary as "the Dear Boy" or "Our Western Wanderer."

Martha "Mattie" Griffith
Browne (1828–1906), Albert G.
Browne's wife
A strong-willed, Kentucky-born abolitionist
and novelist, she married Browne in 1867
in New York. *Mathew Brady photo courtesy of
Browne family descendant Katherine Greenough.*

that region's shortage of eligible women. It was an offbeat effort at social intervention worthy of Brigham Young in the adjoining territory to Oregon's south.[36]

Immediately after the war, Browne spent several years as the official "reporter" (editor/publisher) for the decisions of the Supreme Judicial Court of Massachusetts. In 1867 he married Martha ("Mattie") Griffith, formerly of Kentucky. Although they would reside in Cambridge, the ceremony was performed in New York by a Presbyterian minister, with the bride a Roman Catholic and the groom a Unitarian given to anti-Mormonism. Pre-war Griffith had caused a sensation with her outspoken abolitionism, a commitment that had led her to move to Philadelphia. There, in 1856, she completed a book titled *Autobiography of a Female Slave* and published it using the pseudonym "Ann." With the proceeds from this volume and additional fundraising, she returned to Kentucky long enough to free her six inherited slaves. The

36   "Too Many Women in the East," essay, April 17, 2014, website of Clackamas County Historical Society, Oregon City, Oregon, www.clackamascountyhistoricalsociety.wordpress.com, accessed August 14, 2020.

book was reviled in the South but was well-received elsewhere until Griffith revealed that she was the author—a Caucasian abolitionist not a fugitive slave. An uproar ensued in literary and political circles over the propriety of such a ruse. During 1859–60 Mattie Griffith spent time in Boston to bring off the publication of her second novel, *Madge Vertner*; it was perhaps there she met her future husband. What role, if any, the example of Mattie Griffith's writing played in Albert's later decision to publish *The Ward of the Three Guardians* is an intriguing unknown.[37]

In 1869 the Brownes moved from the Boston area to Manhattan, where Albert became an editor at first the New York *Evening Post* and then the *New York Herald*. His wife continued her work on behalf of America's freedmen while becoming part of the women's suffrage movement. At the *Herald* proprietor James Gordon Bennett involved Albert in the newspaper's international affairs. In 1882 Browne traveled to Mexico, and in 1883 Bennett sent both Brownes to South America to report on the War of the Pacific between Chile and Peru. Albert later lectured and published about the dangers of Chile's growing naval power. There were vague but unsubstantiated hints that the Brownes' South American trip involved intelligence gathering, and, after Albert's death, Mattie Browne alluded to a murky episode in Chile during which her husband was briefly held captive: "In that little

37   Unattributed [Martha Griffith], *Autobiography of a Female Slave* (New York: Redfield, 1857). In her second novel *Madge Vertner* Griffith altered the names of several slaves and one slaveholder much as Albert was to do later in *Ward*. This was notable in the case of Stephen Bishop, a nationally famous slave who worked as a tour guide at Kentucky's Mammoth Cave, an attraction which Albert Browne (and Mattie Griffith before him) visited in 1857. In her novel Griffith altered the name of Bishop's owner, Dr. John Croghan, to "Sam Hemingway." Joe Lockard, " 'A Light Broke Out Over My Mind': Madge Vertner, and Kentucky Abolitionism," *Filson History Quarterly* 76 (Summer 2002), 259–60. For biographical sketches see also: Lockard, "Afterword," in Mattie Griffith, *Autobiography of a Female Slave* (Jackson, Miss.: Banner Books, 1998 reprint), 403–18; Larry Ceplair, "Mattie Griffith Browne: A Kentucky Abolitionist," *Filson Club History Quarterly* 68 (April 1994): 219–31.

wooden shelter where the Chileans imprisoned him he towered miles above his confreres and persecutors, with never a word of reproach or blame against his persecutors."[38]

During 1887 the Brownes returned to Boston. Whether this move was prompted by the death of Albert's father two years earlier or fatigue over his duties at the *Herald* is unknown. In October of 1886, a British house guest at Albert's home on East 19th Street described his daily work routine: "As Mr. Browne's occupation was to summarize all the evening papers for the morning's issue, his work was from midnight till four in the morning. Then all the forenoon he had to do the same thing with the morning papers for the evening issue, getting his sleep in the early morning and afternoon."[39] Once back in Boston, Albert entered the banking firm of Cordley & Co., continued active in the affairs of Harvard '53, and became a Boston clubman, albeit one with declining health and mobility. Albert Browne died in 1891 of what his widow termed a "virulent" case of diabetes at age fifty-six.

❧ PETER K. DOTSON

Notwithstanding the title of Browne's novella, Peter Dotson, the U.S. marshal for Utah, was the sole person Judge Eckels appointed as Henrietta Polydore's guardian in August 1858.

---

38 Martha Griffith Browne, undated holograph biographical sketch, Albert G. Browne File, Records of the [Harvard] Class of 1853 Secretary. If indeed A. G. Browne was gathering intelligence about Chilean naval capabilities in the early 1880s, this would be consistent with his willingness to undertake confidential missions for General Johnston and Governor Andrew in 1858 and 1861, respectively. Albert G. Browne, Jr., "The Growing Power of the Republic of Chile," *Journal of the American Geographical Society of New York* 16 (1884): 1–88. For tensions over the balance of naval power along the Pacific Coast of the Americas during the 1880s, see William F. Sater, "Chile Confronts the United States, 1884–1891," in *Chile and the United States: Empires in Conflict* (Athens: University of Georgia Press, 1990), 51–68.

39 Alfred Russell Wallace, *My Life, A Record of Events and Opinions.* 2 vols. (London: Chapman & Hill, 1905) 2: 108.

Messrs. Browne and McCormick joined Dotson in this role, but did so only informally, by virtue of their friendship with him, and their recent engagement as Henry Polydore's attorney-proxies. With *Ward's* description of Dotson as a Civil War casualty of unknown allegiance, it is clear that by 1877 Browne had lost track of him, thus resorting to fabrication as a means of explaining while romanticizing the marshal's post-Utah fate. Dotson, a Virginian by birth, served in the army of neither the United States nor the Confederacy, although folklore in the Pueblo, Colorado area describes "Uncle Pete" as sympathetic to southern guerillas operating there; he died in his own bed.

After Judge Eckels returned east in mid-September 1858, Brigham Young hoped the marshal "will speedily follow in his wake."[40] But Peter Dotson continued on for almost another year in his high-profile role as the tip of the spear for the U.S. government's attempt to restore federal authority in Utah Territory. During that period, the substantial frustrations and hostility that accompanied this effort as well as the punishing financial burden of a legal judgment against him engineered by Brigham Young, overwhelmed Dotson.

In his August 1, 1859, letter of resignation, the marshal delivered a parting blast to President Buchanan stressing the inadequacy of his support for federal appointees:

> I deem it my duty to warn you, so far as my humble voice will avail, that the present policy of the Government towards this Territory will be fatal to Federal supremacy in Utah, and can only tend to build up, consolidate and perpetuate the political and ecclesiastical power of Brigham Young and his successors. The

40   Brigham Young to Thomas L. Kane, September 10, 1858, Matthew J. Grow and Ronald W. Walker, eds., *The Prophet and the Reformer: The Letters of Brigham Young and Thomas L. Kane* (New York: Oxford University Press, 2015), 295.

unasked and to this day derided [April 6, 1858] pardon extended [by you] to treason has only tended to encourage traitors; and the presence of Federal troops, crippled and humiliated by the instructions and restraints imposed on them serves only the purpose of enriching the coffers of the Mormon Church and of subserving the ends of Mormon polity. The Courts of the United States in the Territory [are] powerless to do good . . . The Federal officers . . . are as forms without substance, shadows without reality. Though willing to serve the Administration from which I received my appointment, I cannot remain an officer of the government without the power to maintain its dignity.[41]

With the unpleasantries of Utah behind him, Dotson moved to Pueblo, Colorado. There he threw in with legendary rancher Charles Goodnight, acquired a gigantic cattle spread derived from the Nolan Mexican Land Grant along the upper St. Charles River, ran a boarding house, became a short-line railroad developer, and died in 1898 at age seventy-five as one of the region's most respected citizens. In his later years, "Uncle Pete" liked to reprise his role in escorting "Brig" to a federal courtroom in Salt Lake City packed with Young's heavily armed "b'hoys." Although Peter K. Dotson did not die during 1864 in Virginia's Battle of the Wilderness, as Albert Browne ambiguously had it, he nonetheless felt he had fought a campaign along the Wasatch Front during the 1850s.[42]

---

41   Peter K. Dotson to James Buchanan, August 1, 1859, "Marshal Dotson's Resignation Letter," *Deseret News*, November 9, 1859.

42   A. A. Hayes, Jr., "The Cattle Ranches of Colorado," *Harper's Monthly*, November 1879, 877–96; H. H. Bancroft, "Doings of Peter K. Dotson," 1884 interview, holograph notes, Bancroft Library, University of California, Berkeley; "From Mace's Hole, the Way It Was, To Beulah, the Way It Is," *A Comprehensive History of Beulah, Colorado* (Colorado Springs: Beulah Historical Society, 2000 rev. ed.); "Peter K. Dotson, a Pioneer, Passed Away last Night Aged Seventy-Five Years," *Pueblo [Colorado] Daily Chieftain*, July 7, 1898; Eleanor Fry, *Peter K. Dotson: Federal Marshal, Rancher, 1823–1898* (Pueblo, Colo.: Pueblo County Historical Society, 2004).

⚜ WASHINGTON JAY McCORMICK

After all of the other principals in the Henrietta Polydore case left Utah, Washington J. McCormick remained. No longer a federal appointee, he practiced law in Salt Lake City among the territory's growing non-Mormon population rather than return to Indiana with Judge Eckels. In the early 1860s he moved north to Montana Territory with several other civilian veterans of the Utah War to pan for gold in what became the Virginia City area. Later, McCormick helped found Missoula and became one of Montana's leading attorneys, entrepreneurs, and territorial legislators. He died prematurely at age fifty-three in 1889 after being blown off a roof in a freak gale that struck Fort Owen, a Fort Bridger–like McCormick property in the Bitter Root Valley near Missoula. He left behind a sterling reputation as well as a five-year-old namesake, who in the early twentieth century became one of Montana's U.S. senators.[43] Remnants of the McCormick family and its philanthropic legacy remain in the Missoula area.

⚜ DELANA R. ECKELS

After depositing Henrietta Polydore with Lord Napier at the British Legation in Washington and pleading his case for greater support with the Buchanan administration, Judge Eckels returned home to Greencastle. There he contemplated his future and presumably made arrangements for the two other young women he had brought out of Utah with Henrietta: Elizabeth Cotton and Mary Tecumbiats. In the spring of 1859, Eckels set out for Utah to resume his role at the head of the territory's judiciary. Instead

---

43   There is no biography of McCormick, although his Montana years are documented in Washington J. McCormick Papers, Mansfield Library, University of Montana, Missoula; and Montana Historical Society, Helena.

of bringing with him his wife, as originally intended, Eckels recruited as companions a small cadre of young Hoosier lawyers—just as he had traveled west with Washington J. McCormick in 1857.[44] Once back in the territory, Judge Eckels again plunged into controversy. Interestingly, he remained in some way in the thoughts of Jane Mayer Richards, who, from the distance of the Mayer family cotton farm in Arkansas, inquired "how he is getting along &c" in a letter to her husband, who had returned to Utah from Great Britain in the spring of 1858. As discussed above, Samuel W. Richards responded to Jane's query about the judge with comments that were consistently negative, a hostility no doubt fueled by Eckels' disclosure to Jane that, in her absence, Samuel had taken a sixth wife. In 1861, after participating in some of the sensational legal jousts wracking Utah over territorial and federal jurisdictional matters and the power of judges to sanction use of federal troops, Eckels resigned and returned again to Indiana.

In Greencastle, Eckels was active in Democratic Party politics but sat out the Civil War as an openly Southern sympathizer or "Copperhead." In 1863 he saw his son, William, marry Elizabeth Cotton a few days after divorce from his first wife. Like his protege McCormick in Montana, Judge Eckels died a violent death following a carriage accident in 1888 at age eighty-two.

---

44 Eckels mentioned his intent to have his wife accompany him back to Utah in the spring of 1859 to William A. Carter when he and his entourage stopped briefly at Fort Bridger during the last week of September 1858. During that encounter Eckels delegated to Carter his responsibilities as a judge of the U.S. district court in Utah, an unusual arrangement since Carter was only a non-attorney justice of the peace for Utah's Green River County. Carter (Fort Bridger) to Mary E. Carter (Columbia, Mo.), September 26 and December 9, 1858, typescript of 1955 (pp. 18 and 25), William A. Carter Papers, BANC MSS 99/75, The Bancroft Library, University of California, Berkeley.

Apparently both men went to their graves without revealing that during 1857–58 they had sent dispatches from the Utah Expedition to the Cincinnati *Enquirer* under the pen names "Kenton" and "Kenton, Jr."[45]

❧ THE WARD OF THE THREE GUARDIANS: ITS FATE

It could be argued that when Albert Browne's novella appeared in the June 1877 issue of *The Atlantic Monthly* it should have created a stir in literary and perhaps political circles. As discussed above, Browne wrote during a period of peak national interest, if not outrage, over Utah and Mormon affairs.

Notwithstanding this topicality, *Ward* drew minimal attention. Newspapers throughout the country took notice of it, but only in a sentence or two as part of a listing of the articles contained in *The Atlantic's* new issue. None of them explained who A. G. Browne was or why he wrote. The Salt Lake City newspapers, including the *Deseret News*, ignored the piece entirely, as did Browne's own employer (the *New York Herald*) and the nearby *New-York Tribune*, the paper that sent him to Utah twenty years earlier. The editors have found no substantive review or analysis of *Ward* in literary magazines. It is emblematic that in her diary Albert's mother mentioned *Ward* only briefly and Henrietta Polydore's name not at all. She seemed to confuse the novella with her son's earlier three-part essay for *The Atlantic Monthly*

---

45   For Eckels' return journey to Utah and later life, see Richard Wiles Jones, Diary, April 19–August 30, 1859, Special Collections, Roy O. West Library, DePauw University, Greencastle, Indiana; Eckels file, compiled by Virginia C. Brann, Local History Department, Putnam County Public Library, Greencastle; Nicole Etcheson, "Repudiating the Administration: The Copperheads in Putnam County, Indiana," *Ohio Valley History* 13 (Fall 2013): 46–64.

of 1859: "Read Albert's article upon the Utah Expedition which interested me much. The style is easy & graceful. It was a most perilous undertaking, full of hardship & suffering."[46]

Historians too ignored the novella until a brief first mention of it in an article for the *Journal of Mormon History* in 2003, 126 years after it appeared. Thirteen more years passed before a monograph mentioned the Henrietta Polydore case and the related existence of *The Ward of the Three Guardians*.[47]

Why such neglect? Perhaps most obvious is the fact that neither Browne nor William Dean Howells, his editor, made any apparent effort to draw attention to *Ward*. In 1877 Browne and Howells were literally surrounded by Manhattan and Boston publishers, but there are no signs that they used their strategic perches to secure reviews for *Ward*. From a twenty-first-century perspective, this self-defeating effacement seemed to go beyond the genteel authorial and editorial norms of the era, especially considering the amount of time and effort Browne invested in creating *Ward*.

Compounding this passivity was the novella's opaque title, which did little to signal potential readers that it connected to such topical issues as Utah, Mormons, or polygamy. For those who bought it and actually started into Browne's work, it was

---

46 Diary of Sarah Smith Cox Browne, May 25, 1877, Browne Family Papers, MC 298, Schlesinger Library, Radcliffe Institute. Interestingly, her 1859 diary comments about Albert's earlier piece in *The Atlantic Monthly* were even more terse.

47 MacKinnon, "Epilogue to the Utah War: Impact and Legacy," *Journal of Mormon History* 29 (Fall 2003): 231–34; Stephen L. Prince, *Hosea Stout: Lawman, Legislator, Mormon Defender* (Logan: Utah State University Press, 2016), 279–80. In 1964 historian Juanita Brooks edited and published the diary of Jane Mayer Richards' defense attorney, Hosea Stout, and included Stout's summary of the Polydore case's origins and outcome without reference to the related subsequent publication of Browne's novella. See Juanita Brooks, ed., *On the Mormon Frontier*, 2: 662–63 (August 2–4, 1858).

necessary to read three-quarters of the novella before understanding the meaning of its title. (Even today, *Ward*'s title ren-
ders it inaccessible to researchers who interrogate internet search
engines using these key words.) To the extent that in 1877 *The
Atlantic*'s subscribers still remembered the Polydore case, the
fact that Browne altered Henrietta's surname to "Perego" without explanation did nothing to stimulate readership or resonance
among that group. This matter of disguising identities in 1877 is
an especially puzzling one when one considers that Browne had
already used the proper surnames of Henry, Henrietta, Samuel,
and Jane in his coverage of the Polydore legal case for the *Tribune*
as a news item in 1858.[48]

The editors are not arguing that Browne and *The Atlantic
Monthly* should have "puffed" *Ward* by using a sensational title
like those Fanny Stenhouse selected for her two books in 1872
and 1874—*Expose of Polygamy in Utah: A Lady's Life among the
Mormons* and *"Tell It All": The Story of a Life's Experience in Mormonism*—but the metaphor of a light hidden beneath a bushel
basket comes to mind. The title A. G. Browne and his editor
selected is understandable once one has read the full story, but
it virtually condemned the piece to obscurity. The Rossettis, the
surviving Polydores, and their British friends, had they realized
what Browne published in 1877, might have judged its title "clever
by more than half."

---

48   For the original (1858) use of his characters' real names, see [Browne] "Later from
    Utah, Dispatch, August 5, 1858, *New-York Tribune*, September 6, 1858, 6/1–2.

Editors' Conclusions

$\mathcal{G}$IVEN THE FOREGOING, WHAT CONCLUSIONS MIGHT one draw about *Ward* and its significance? Five major ones come to mind.

☙ A COMPLEX TALE OF ITS TIMES, LAMENTABLY FORGOTTEN

First, *The Ward of the Three Guardians* was very much a dramatic, colorful story of its time but a complex one lamentably forgotten. Browne wrote in 1877, a time of intense interest in Utah and the Latter-day Saints but did so by focusing on the events of twenty years earlier when the country as a whole was beginning its bloody slide into disunion. The span of time challenges the reader to stay with the very long chain of events then called "the Mormon problem." Adding to this structural complexity, Browne chose to do this through a mixture of fact and fiction, forcing the reader to cope with significant ambiguities and gaps in the story, while avoiding the pitfalls of Browne's episodic forays into complete fantasy.

With the advent of the non-fiction novel in the 1960s, modern readers are partially equipped to deal with such a challenge, but those of the Victorian era may have struggled. Early enthusiasts of what became the Sherlock Holmes canon had to deal with much the same issue in Conan Doyle's realistic portrayal of fog-shrouded London juxtaposed with his largely fictive rendering of a violent Utah Territory in *A Study in Scarlet*. In a sense, Browne wrote only part way through resolution of the Mormon problem, not at its conclusion. It would take another twenty years after *Ward*'s publication for Utah to gain statehood, and another two decades beyond that landmark for the country to welcome her into the Union fully. In many respects the "Reconstruction" of Utah following the Utah War was longer and as tumultuous as that besetting the eleven states of the Confederacy after the Civil War. The appearance of *Ward* in 1877 was a literary way station in this agonizing saga, not the complete story of how it unfolded.

Compounding *Ward*'s structural complexity was the impact of selecting a convoluted title for Browne's story and the alteration of several of its central characters' names. Certain aspects of that choice, made by either the author or his editor, William Dean Howells, did little to keep it before the reading public or to attract the later interest of historians. Obscured in the process were several aspects of the Utah War's colorful story unavailable elsewhere. *Ward*'s account of Albert Browne's 2,000-mile eastbound winter trek from Fort Bridger to Washington fills a gap worth understanding along with the plight of Henrietta Polydore, one masked by her appearance in *Ward* as a girl dubbed "Perego."

⚜ WOMEN'S INVOLVEMENT: HOME FRONT AND BIVOUAC

Second, the novella's focus on the adventures of twelve-year-old Henrietta and her plucky female relatives serves to remind that the Utah War was a conflict involving women and girls on both sides as well as men and boys. For every eleven-year-old Billy

Kelly struggling to survive in the midst of the army's Utah Expedition, there was an Augusta Joyce Crocheron, the thirteen-year-old Latter-day Saint who, with her parents, shielded Thomas L. Kane from a lynch mob in San Bernardino so that he might reach the Salt Lake Valley to mediate the war.[1]

If this observation seems obvious in today's environment of universal women's suffrage, equal opportunity, and female fighter pilots, such was not always the case. As recently as 1959, the gender imbalance in historical focus (and even on history faculties) was such that Professor David M. Potter, Yale's ranking historian, felt impelled to deliver a public address titled "American Women and the American Character." In these remarks Potter lamented that "our social generalizations [including those of historians] is mainly in masculine terms." He argued, "what we say about the character of the American people should be said not in

---

1   Kelly had been hired in Independence during the spring of 1857 for light duty by W. M. F. Magraw's Pacific Wagon Road crew to tend its small odometer wagon. At Fort Laramie a drunken soldier shot Kelly, who recovered and continued west to spend the winter at the bivouac his crew built in the Wind River Mountains along the Popo Agie River near South Pass. Vulnerable to attack by both the Nauvoo Legion and Crows, Gen. Johnston ordered this isolated group to relocate to the relative safety of Camp Scott in March 1858. There Billy Kelly did odd chores as a civilian. Young Kelly's presence in the midst of the Utah Expedition may have unwittingly inspired the bogus story circulated by Bill Cody twenty years later that he had spent the winter of 1858 at Fort Bridger as an eleven-year-old assistant teamster under the protection of James Butler ("Wild Bill") Hickok. For Kelly's background and mishap at Fort Laramie, see Frederick W. Lander to Col. William Hoffman and Hoffman to Lander, July 4 and 5, 1857, as well as Lander to W. M. F. Magraw, July 6, all in Letterbook, Vol. 12 (April 30, 1857–March 22, 1858), Container 9, Frederick W. Lander Collection, Library of Congress. For Cody's later fabrication about a youthful involvement with the Utah Expedition, see MacKinnon, ed., *At Sword's Point, Part 1*, 355, 357–58. Augusta Joyce Crocheron's interactions with Thomas L. Kane, are described in MacKinnon, *Across the Desert in 1858: Thomas L. Kane's Mediating Mission and the Mormon Women Who Made It Possible*, 35th Annual Juanita Brooks Lecture (St. George, Ut.: Dixie State University Library, 2018).

terms of half of the American population—even if it is the male half—but in terms of the character of the totality of the people. . . . [A]ttention to the historic character of American women is important not only as a specialty . . . but as a coordinate major part of the overall comprehensive study of the American character as a whole."[2] One of us (MacKinnon) was Potter's student in his small senior seminar when he delivered this lecture more than sixty years ago, and can vouch for the likelihood that, had he then been aware of Henrietta Polydore's story, Professor Potter might well have included it in the syllabus for Yale's History 90.[3]

At the beginning of this book, we noted the extent to which women in Brigham Young's extended family—especially Eliza Roxcy Snow and Susa Young Gates—contributed morale-building poems or faith-promoting novels connected to the Utah War. That was the least of it. Other, less genteel Latter-day Saint women participated in the war too. They did so on a grittier level by clothing and provisioning the troops of the Nauvoo Legion and the Standing Army of Israel—thousands of them—while providing for the children and grandparents they so-abruptly left behind, often with inadequate support. It was a herculean effort made by a hardscrabble population of women, girls, and boys often within one hundred twenty miles of the front lines at Camp Scott. Such work enabled their families to survive the brutal winter of 1858 and the disruptive ordeal of the Move South that followed in the snow and sleet of spring.

---

2   For the text of Potter's 1959 lecture delivered at Florida's Stetson University, see Don E. Fehrenbacher, ed., *History and American Society: Essays of David M. Potter* (New York: Oxford University Press, 1973), 277–303.

3   In 1959, Potter was Yale's Sterling Professor of History. Although often identified with research and writing about the American South and the coming of the Civil War, his first book was about the West, and his last years were spent teaching in California at Stanford University.

Typical of the burdens borne on the home front were those of Ann Oades Jackson while her husband, a Legionnaire, campaigned with Maj. Lot Smith's famous detachment of raiders in Echo Canyon and near Fort Bridger during the fall of 1857. For Pvt. Henry Clark Jackson, military service in the field was more of a lark than serious church business, but for his wife, living in Salt Lake City, it was a nightmarish experience:

> When I tell you how I have fared you will at once no doubt forgive me [for not writing] for the children have all been sick. . . . I have been up night and day all most for they was worse in the night. You would have though[t] they could not breathe. To help them I [?] put them in warm baths. I was taken with the same complaint on wednesday last and have not been able to write since I got your letter before to day for my head [h]as been so bad that I could not look steady at any thing long. So you see the way I live and my hands full since you left me and I have had no one to do the first thing for me. I am alone day and night. . . . Well I am glad to hear that you look so well and that you have enjoyed your self since you have been out but I would be more glad if you had got through there and got home. I hope you will not be much longer . . . I wish I had something good to send you but I have not but I pray that the Lord God of Israel will bless you . . . there is no wood come yet. Excuse all blunders.[4]

When Brigham Young announced on March 21, 1858, that tens of thousands of mothers like Mrs. Jackson were to bundle up their possessions and families, prepare their homes for incineration, and flee south in winter weather to an unknown destination, the strain on their faith and church discipline grew commensurately. Take, for example, the situation of Cynthia Jane Park Stowell, a

---

4 Ann Oades Jackson to Henry Clark Jackson, October 18, 1857, Ward Jay Roylance Collection, Church History Library.

plural wife of Lt. William R. R. Stowell, the Legion adjutant captured by the Utah Expedition in October 1857 and still imprisoned at Camp Scott under a federal treason indictment. When the Move South was launched, Cynthia Stowell was in the last stages of pregnancy and overwhelmed by the responsibility of caring for at least thirteen children and the uncertainty of her absent husband's fate. On April 14, 1858, she delivered her baby, and, after only a week of rest, headed south with a sister wife and their large brood aboard a wagon pulled by two yokes of steers.[5]

The weight of the Move South also fell heavily on the children involved, impacting them in ways obscured by more than 160 years of faith-promoting folklore and upbeat war stories. One unidentified girl, age eleven, found it deeply unsettling to leave her home—ready for the torch—for the uncertainties of life on the road:

> There were seven of us children in the family. We put away all our playthings, for the days found us so frightened that all we did was to follow father and mother from place to place, looking into their faces for a word of comfort and a look of cheer. One morning father told us that we should leave with a large company in the evening. He said little more. There was packing and the making of bread. Along in the middle of the day father scattered leaves and straw in all the rooms and through my tears I heard him say 'Never mind, little daughter, this home has sheltered us, it shall never shelter them.' I did not understand him then, but as we went out of the yard and joined all the other people on the main road I learned for the first time that the city was to be burned should the approaching army attack the people. That night we camped on Willow Creek. . . . I cried and cried, but at last I dropped to sleep.[6]

---

5   Devon R. Jensen and Kenneth L. Alford, " 'I was not ready to die yet': William Stowell's Utah War Ordeal," BYU *Studies Quarterly* 56, no. 4 (Fall 2017): 29–52.

6   Reminiscense of unidentified girl in Levi Edgar Young, *Chief Episodes in the History of Utah* (Chicago: The Lakeside Press, 1912), 34–35.

At the army's winter quarters along Blacks Fork of the Green River, women shared the troops' hardships, although they did so bivouacked in tents and crude log huts at an altitude of 7,000 feet above sea level rather than in the more comfortable adobe brick houses of the Salt Lake Valley. It was not quite the Valley Forge experience of eighty years earlier, but with temperatures as much as twenty degrees below freezing and firewood available only at a distance of ten miles or more, it was an experience they remembered for the rest of their lives.

The size and character of the female population at Camp Scott is not well understood, but we know that it included the wives of four officers, perhaps as many as eighty company laundresses (often the spouses of the command's sergeants), and Elizabeth Wells Randall Cumming, the patrician wife of Utah's new governor. Mrs. Cumming, a descendant of the Revolution's Samuel Adams, acted as the governor's confidential secretary while nursing a foot badly frost-bitten during her participation in the daunting march from Fort Laramie to Fort Bridger.[7]

The woman most put to the test on the war's federal side was Jenny Goodale, the Shoshone wife of one of the army's civilian guides, Tim Goodale. She accompanied the small detachment Capt. Randolph B. Marcy led down the spine of the Continental Divide from Fort Bridger to New Mexico to buy thousands of mules and horses to remount the Utah Expedition. Marcy's was the longest, most arduous winter march in American military history until the epic retreat from North Korea's Chosin Reservoir during the winter of 1951. Jenny Goodale survived the

---

7   MacKinnon, ed., *At Sword's Point, Part 2*, 564. Audrey M. Godfrey, "Housewives, Hussies, and Heroines: The Women with Johnston's Army," *Utah Historical Quarterly* 54 (Spring 1986): 157–78; Elizabeth Wells Randall Cumming, *The Genteel Gentile: Letters of Elizabeth Cumming, 1857–1858*, ed. by Ray R. Canning and Beverly Beeton (Salt Lake City: Tanner Trust Fund, University of Utah Library, 1977).

1,600-mile trek to New Mexico and back, although her favorite pony—eaten by troops facing starvation—and Sgt. William H. Morton did not.[8]

Latter-day Saint women also endured long treks during the Utah War's winter weather, although they were not the ordeal Jenny Goodale experienced. When Brigham Young set out in April 1857 on a 1,000-mile journey through snow and across frozen streams to inspect Fort Limhi, the Latter-day Saint Indian mission and Nauvoo Legion post on Oregon Territory's Salmon River, he took with him a total of 142 people, twenty-one of whom were women, including three of his own wives. When, with army complicity, a band of 200 Northern Shoshone and Bannock warriors attacked Fort Limhi on February 25, 1858—ten months after Brigham Young's party returned to Salt Lake City—women were among the garrison's defenders but not among its dead and wounded.[9]

The women in the middle of this unprecedented territorial-federal conflict were also caught up as participants, often in quite different ways. The most prominent of these, other than the poet Christina Rossetti, was Elizabeth D. W. Kane of Philadelphia, the twenty-one-year-old, English-born wife of Thomas L. Kane. In December 1857 it fell to Elizabeth, a Protestant deeply suspicious of Brigham Young and Mormonism, to defend before her husband's skeptical family his gratuitous decision to travel

8   For the story of the Marcy trek and Jenny Goodale's participation within the context of the Utah War, see MacKinnon, ed., " 'Great Disaster Might Befall the Command': War Spreads to New Mexico," At Sword's Point, Part 2, 38–64. For Jenny's elusive later years and those of her husband, see James W. McGill, Rediscovered Frontiersman, Timothy Goodale (Independence, Mo.: Oregon-California Trails Association, 2009).

9   David L. Bigler, "Mormon Missionaries, the Utah War, and the 1858 Bannock Raid on Fort Limhi," Montana The Magazine of Western History 53 (Autumn 2005): 30–43, and Fort Limhi: The Mormon Adventure in Oregon Territory, 1855–1858 (Spokane, Wash.: The Arthur H. Clark Co., 2003), 134–60, 331–33.

to Utah in the dead of winter to mediate the Utah War. Elizabeth recognized that her husband viewed such a mission as a calling, and she hoped that performing it would bolster his recent acceptance of Christianity (at her urging) after a life of agnosticism. And so at year-end 1857 Tom Kane resigned his clerkship in his father's court—his sole source of income—and, after making scant financial provision for his wife and two young children (who were to room with his elderly parents), set out for Utah on a mission of unknown duration with uncertain outcome on behalf of a reviled people whose religion he did not accept. Although the Kane family was patrician and land rich, in 1858 it was essentially cash poor. All during Thomas' free-spending absence in the West, Elizabeth led a life of extreme penury, a circumstance aggravated by the death of Judge Kane on February 21, 1858, just as Tom reached Salt Lake City, and the subsequent victimization of his widow by a family financial advisor.[10]

In 1859 Apostle Wilford Woodruff paid tribute to the sacrifices made by Elizabeth Kane so that her husband might pursue his adventures in the West. In writing to Tom Kane, Woodruff observed, "The goodness of heart and kindness of Mrs. Kane and the sacrifice she made, in encouraging and assisting her companion to undertake a long and perilous journey to aid in delivering a calumniated people from the horror of war, have often been a topic of conversation in the social circles of the ladies of Deseret."[11] It is our view that few of today's students of the Utah War—focused

---

10 MacKinnon, ed., *At Sword's Point, Part 1*, 500–12, and *Part 2*, 187–213, 275–308, 495–50.

11 Wilford Woodruff to Thomas L. Kane, March 8, 1859, Historian's Office Letterpress Copybooks, Vol. 1 (1854–1861), 727–30: CR 100/38, Church History Library. For more insight into Elizabeth's complex view of Latter-day Saints, see Darcee Barnes, "Elizabeth Kane's 'Mormon Problem': Another Perspective of Thomas L. Kane's Work for the Mormons," *Journal of Mormon History* 43 (July 2017): 68–95.

primarily on Thomas Kane's dramatic role—recognize the extent and importance of his wife's wartime contributions. In justice to Elizabeth Kane, more historians need to recognize and acknowledge what Apostle Woodruff saw in this remarkable woman.

Interestingly, nearly a year before Henrietta Mayer Polydore journeyed to New York Harbor to see her daughter off for Liverpool on the last leg of her repatriation to England, Elizabeth Kane traveled to the same port to see her husband board S.S. *Moses Taylor* for the first segment of his mission to Utah via Panama and California. Both ladies, English by birth but American by choice, had a role to play as the Utah War engulfed their loved one.

Most unfortunate of those caught in the middle of the Utah War were the emigrants of the Baker-Fancher party, who unwittingly became victims of mass murder at Mountain Meadows in southern Utah while en route to California. Will Bagley, one of the historians most knowledgeable about the massacre, estimates that more than 60 percent of the approximately 120 people killed on September 11, 1857, were women and children, some only infants. It was their deaths ("innocent blood") that weighed most heavily on Brigham Young when he learned what had happened at Mountain Meadows, but many modern historians lose sight of the atrocity's gender implications, fixated as they are on the total body count and the continuing search for leader accountability.[12] It was the point David Potter made in his thoughtful lecture one hundred years later.

If during Samuel W. Richards' long absence from Salt Lake City during 1857–58 Henrietta Polydore experienced the discomforts

---

12   Will Bagley, *Blood of the Prophets: Brigham Young and the Massacre at Mountain Meadows* (Norman: University of Oklahoma Press, 2002); Ronald W. Walker, Richard E. Turley Jr., and Glen M. Leonard, *Massacre at Mountain Meadows* (New York: Oxford University Press, 2008).

of food and fuel shortages, and if she did indeed participate in the upheaval of the Move South—Brigham Young's attempt to conduct a retreat (possibly to northern Mexico), a decision over which he expressed rare public doubt[13]—she had plenty of company, much of it female. Oh, that we could know how Henrietta described these experiences on the American frontier to her Rossetti cousins once back in the over-heated drawing rooms of Victorian England. Unfortunately, even Albert Browne's fertile imagination did not rise to that challenge.

⚜ A REGIONAL, CONTINENTAL, AND INTERNATIONAL CONFLICT

Henrietta Polydore's Anglo-Italian background alone signals that the armed conflict that surrounded her was hardly one limited to Washington, D.C. and Utah Territory. But for those who approach her story carefully, there are additional reminders of a context with immense scope and sweep. After all, Elder Samuel W. Richards of Massachusetts, patriarch of the household in

13   During a lengthy March 21, 1858 address in the adobe Salt Lake tabernacle during which he publicly announced the Move South, Young said, "Many may say, 'br. Brigham, perhaps you are mistaken; you are liable to err, and if the mob should not come, after all, and we should burn up our houses and learn that the Government had actually countermanded their orders and that no armies are coming to Utah, it would be a needless destruction. We have all the time felt that there was no need of leaving our houses. How easy it is for men to be mistaken, and we think a Prophet may be mistaken once in a while.' I am just as willing as the Lord, if he is disposed to make me make mistakes, and it is none of the business of any other person. . . . And if the Lord wants me to make a mistake, I would as soon be mistaken as anything else, if that will save the lives of the people and give us the victory. If you get such feelings in your hearts, think of what my conclusion on the subject is, and do not come to my office to ask me whether I am mistaken, for I want to tell you now perhaps I am." In Richard S. Van Wagoner, *The Complete Discourses of Brigham Young, Volume 3—1857 to 1861* (Salt Lake City: The Smith-Pettit Foundation, 2009), 1858.

which Henrietta hid as "Lucy," had served in the British Mission three times and, as did Henrietta, crossed the Atlantic to do so at least six times. In Richards' case, what went with each of his trans-Atlantic voyages was a 2,000-mile overland trek between the Great Basin and the Atlantic Coast. All of this travel came during an era when most Americans and British subjects never left their home county. That Henrietta's sojourn in Salt Lake City took place among five sister wives (including her aunt Jane), all of whom were born in England, and that a large percentage of the Latter-day Saints who surrounded them in Utah were native to Great Britain, Germany, and Scandinavia rather than the United States, adds a fine point to their own non-American origins.

When one considers that more than half of the Utah Expedition's troops had also been born outside of the United States, one again realizes *Ward*'s international context. Some of these soldiers, as well as their adversaries in the Nauvoo Legion, were veterans of the British Army and its recent fighting in the Crimea; one of them, the U.S. Army's Sgt.-Maj. William Porter Finlay, a native of Belfast, had lived in Ireland, England, South Africa's Cape Colony, India, and Australia before immigrating to the United States to campaign against the Latter-day Saints. That both sides in the war also used and show-cased veterans of the Texas Rangers adds to the conflict's polychromatic character.

Not only were the Utah War's participants diverse in their nationality, the geopolitical background against which they campaigned was similarly far-reaching. For example, it would be a mistake to assume that the "Utah" of *The Ward of the Three Guardians* equates to today's smallish, near-rectangular state. To the contrary, when Browne and Polydore were in Utah it was a sprawling entity with borders stretching from the Continental Divide to California's eastern boundary, with counties more than 700 miles wide. It was in part retribution for the war that led Congress to unilaterally reduce Utah Territory's borders six times during the 1860s to reach their present dimensions.

Another reflection of the war's scope and sweep runs to the operational history of the Nauvoo Legion's raids and patrols. Although the Legion was a territorial militia, an organization authorized by Congress to operate only within Utah's borders, Brigham Young dispatched its troops to execute military missions as far afield as the State of California and the territories of Nebraska, New Mexico, and Oregon. So expansive (and ambiguous) were Young's plans that Queen Victoria's Royal Navy diverted part of its Pacific Squadron from Peru to pre-empt anticipated Legion landings on Vancouver's Island and in Honolulu Harbor. Politically, because of the vulnerability of their Pacific Coast possessions to Mormon encroachment, Russia authorized negotiations to sell Alaska to the United States in December 1857 and during the following summer Great Britain reorganized the territory administered by the Hudson's Bay Company to form the new Crown Colony of British Columbia.

Similar shock waves impacted defensive planning in Mexico, the Dutch East Indies, Spanish Cuba, and the Caribbean Coast of Central America. If, as the editors believe, Jane Mayer Richards and Henrietta Polydore participated in Brigham Young's Move South during the spring of 1858, they might ultimately have trekked beyond the intermediate destination of Utah County and Provo to a new, ambiguously identified haven in Mexican Sonora. Although such a southern border crossing en mass was not practical and did not happen in 1858, it did take place thirty years later to form the Latter-day Saint *colonias* in Sonora, Chihuahua, and Coahuila. If in Gloucestershire Henry F. Polydore heard the wide-spread rumors of such flight, that as well as fears of a polygamous marriage for his daughter would have propelled him to Lord Malmesbury's foreign ministry to set in motion the chain of events that ultimately led to Albert G. Browne's legal and literary interactions with young Henrietta.

❧ The Perilous World of Polydore and Browne

Browne published *Ward* on the cusp of a great fifty-year era of innovation in the fields of electricity, medicine, mechanical engineering, and personal safety, yet for him and the people about whom he wrote, life remained risky. For them, these potentially life-changing discoveries came too late to make a difference in their longevity.

Henrietta Mayer Polydore, Henry F. Polydore, and Peter K. Dotson may have led long lives, but most of the others in this story died prematurely, falling victim to violent misadventures or chronic diseases now easily treated. Consumption or tuberculosis claimed both young Henrietta in Mississippi and her aunt Jane in Utah at age twenty-eight and thirty-six, respectively; Jane's only child, Phineas Henry Richards, died of unknown cause as a toddler while he and his mother struggled to return to Utah after delivering Henrietta to the Atlantic Coast for repatriation three years earlier. Albert G. Browne was only fifty-six when he died in Boston, an invalid suffering from a diabetic condition his wife and Harvard classmates believed connected to his earlier experiences with the Utah Expedition. Washington J. McCormick died at fifty-three after plunging from a rooftop in frontier Montana, while mentor Judge Eckels lived until age eighty-two when he fell victim to a carriage smash in his beloved Putnam County, Indiana.

In many respects serious illness defined the last years of both A. G. Browne, Jr. and Henrietta Polydore, but the behavior of the two people—author and his protagonist—was quite different. One chose an active life that plunged him into the American Civil War, a controversial marriage, the rough and tumble of Manhattan journalism, and risky travel across wartime South America. The other led a cloistered life of somewhat shabby gentility, limited to shuttling between her warring relatives on two continents in the care of not the Royal Messenger of 1858 but her faithful attendant "Marianne" of the 1860s and 1870s.

During this period, a much-married Brigham Young still seemed to bestride the world of Utah Territory and Mormonism like a colossus, but for him too life was filled with anxiety and precautions. Young experienced constant fear of religious and political persecution, even death by lynch mob of the sort that claimed Joseph Smith in 1844. In the fall of 1857 Albert Browne had carelessly called for such summary judgment in newspaper dispatches distributed across the United States. In 1877, the year Browne published *The Ward of the Three Guardians*, Brigham Young died in his own bed at age seventy-six of a condition misdiagnosed as appendicitis by the physicians he so-long mistrusted. The tone of the society he left was such that the "b'hoys" he had used with great controversy felt compelled to guard his grave each night for months. Young died four months after his religiously adopted son, John D. Lee, met his own fate at Mountain Meadows before a federal firing squad.

By choosing to end *Ward* in Salt Lake City and on a note of British imperial gentility, Albert Browne stepped over the reality that, even in a Victorian Utah linked to the transcontinental railroad and blooming as the rose, life could still be as philosopher Thomas Hobbes saw it—short, mean, and nasty if not

brutish. Battalions of deputy U.S. marshals and army infantry-
men awaited the order to intervene in the daily life of polygamous
Utah. Coercive Reconstruction may have just ended in coastal
Mississippi where Henrietta Polydore lay dead virtually in the
shadow of Jefferson Davis' place of exile, but it was only beginning in the Utah left behind by A. G. Browne's fictive "Henrietta
Perego" and her new husband.

❧ THOUGHTS ON A. G. BROWNE'S ADAPTABILITY

Among the less obvious conclusions one might draw from *Ward*
is what the novella tells us about its author's adaptability. Albert
Browne had the inner strength and coping skills to thrive as
well as survive in settings and under circumstances ranging far
beyond the wildest expectations of most Americans. Fortunately
for posterity, he did so with pen in hand.

Native to a small town of coastal New England and scion to
a genteel family of Protestant merchants linked to China's clipper trade, civilian Browne found himself at age twenty-two in
the midst of North America's so-called Great American Desert,
bivouacked in the midst of America's largest military garrison in
close proximity to the continent's most reviled religious minority.
There, notwithstanding his two Harvard degrees and Heidelberg
Ph.D., Browne became the intimate of the nation's most prominent frontiersman, a roughhewn, illiterate Jim Bridger nicknamed
after the Angel Gabriel. Sustained by his own resourcefulness
and the contents of the carpetbag he had purchased in Germany
two years earlier, Browne generated a tsunami of newspaper dispatches for the celebrated Horace Greeley's *New-York Tribune*.
It was material that in 1859 enabled him to publish a classic,

non-fiction account of the Utah War in the greatest literary journal of the English-speaking world.

In 1877, nearly twenty years later, Browne again published in *The Atlantic Monthly*, this time a novella covering the same campaign's impact on a young Roman Catholic girl caught up in a trans-continental marital and religious dispute involving Latter-day Saints. The editors believe that it was this eclectic background and wealth of experience that permitted A. G. Browne, a distinguished veteran of the Union Army, to add fiction to his repertoire, write *Ward*, and simultaneously edit the *New York Herald*, the world's largest-circulation newspaper. In his spare time, Browne pivoted from these activities to deliver the political coup de grace to Manhattan's notorious William Marcy ("Boss") Tweed.

Writing *The Ward of the Three Guardians* was not the capstone to Browne's career, but it was the direct result of his powers to adapt—his ability to learn and benefit from what he had experienced before confronting even more different writing challenges linked to South America. Whether or not he sensed it, in the 1880s Browne was preparing to meet the agonizing, premature death that overtook him during the next decade in Boston. It was an end not unlike the death in Mississippi of the English youngster whom he had championed as his "ward" in the far-off Salt Lake City of 1858.

Appendices

CHRISTINA G. ROSSETTI (1828–1882)
in 1866 chalk portrait by brother Dante, both cousins of Henrietta Polydore.
Courtesy of Wikimedia Commons.

APPENDIX A

Selected Poetry
by Christina Rossetti

MACKENZIE BELL, ONE OF CHRISTINA ROSSET-
ti's biographers, suggested that "One of the most pleasing of the poems in Christina Rossetti's 'New Poems' is that
addressed 'To Lalla,' the favourite name of her cousin Henrietta
Polydore. The latter was only three years old when the poem was
written. The lines incidentally point the moral that wisdom of
the heart is better than knowledge of the head. It is a trite moral,
but rarely has it been better expressed . . ."

> To Lalla
> Read on: if you knew it
>   You have cause to boast:
> You are much the wiser
>   Though I know the most.[1]

Several pages later, Bell reported that "Christina addressed
to Henrietta Polydore another lyric some years afterwards, the
beautiful poem entitled 'Next of Kin,' dated February 21, 1853.
But here both motive and subject are more in accordance with her

---

1   Mackenzie Bell, *Christina Rossetti: A Biographical and Critical Study*, 4th ed. (London: Thomas Burleigh, 1898), 21–22.

usual manner than is the case in 'To Lalla.' The poem also betokens an expectation of speedy death, which runs through many of her early verses. She addresses her cousin as

> You, white as dove or lily or spirit of the light:
> I, stained and cold and glad to hide in the cold dark night:
> You, joy to many a loving heart and light to many eyes:
> I, lonely in the knowledge earth is full of vanities.

After publishing the poem "Next of Kin," Bell once again mentioned young Henrietta Polydore. "It may, perhaps, be permissible to say here, parenthetically," he wrote, "as showing how early fears may be falsified by fact, that while Christina herself lived an average length of life, and died from a disease far other than that which, in early years, seemed to threaten her, the young lady to whom these poems were addressed died twenty years before her of consumption, the very disease Christina feared for herself when she wrote the poem last named."[2]

---

2   Bell, *Christina Rossetti*, 29.

A Poem by Eliza R. Snow

A Tribute to the Memory of
Mrs. Jane Richards.[1]

A bright and precious jewel,
    From earth is call'd away,
To shine with greater splendor
    In realms of endless day.

We lov'd her cheerful spirit —
    We lov'd her noble heart —
We lov'd her truthful nature,
    And yet, with her must part.

Twere cruel to recall her;
    Our loss, to her is gain;
She's now beyond the province
    Of mortal grief and pain.

To her, death had no terrors —
    Its sting had been remov'd;
The God in whom she trusted,
    In life — in death, she prov'd.

---

1   Jill Mulvay Derr and Karen Lynn Davidson, comps. and eds., *Eliza R. Snow, The Complete Poetry* (Provo and Salt Lake City: BYU Press and University of Utah Press, 2009), 751.

She listen'd to the Gospel,
    Jehovah's sacred truth;
And left the home of childhood,
    And ties of early youth.

In Heav'n she laid up treasures,
    Secure from moth and rust,
Where crowns of life and glory
    Await the pure and just.

G.S.L. City, May 1867 —
Eliza R. Snow.

APPENDIX C

Travels of the Principals

❦ ALBERT G. BROWNE, JR.

1   Salem, Mass. to Ft. Bridger/Camp Scott, U.T. (Summer–Fall 1857, with Utah Expedition) [via rail to N.Y. and St. Louis, Missouri River to Ft. Leavenworth, Oregon/Mormon Trails]

2   Ft. Bridger/Camp Scott to Salem (Winter 1858) [via Oregon/Mormon Trails to Ft. Leavenworth, Missouri River to St. Louis, rail to Salem]

3   Salem to Ft. Bridger/Camp Scott, U.T. (Spring 1858) [via rail to N.Y., Washington, St. Louis, Missouri River to Ft. Leavenworth, Oregon/Mormon Trails]

4   Ft. Bridger/Camp Scott to Salt Lake City (Spring–Summer 1858, with Utah Expedition) [via Mormon Trail and Echo Canyon]

5   Salt Lake City to Salem (Fall 1858) [via Oregon/Mormon Trails to Ft. Leavenworth, Missouri River to St. Louis, rail to Salem]

6   Salem to Washington, D.C. (December 1858) [via rail]

7   Washington, D.C. to Salem (late 1858/early 1859) [via rail]

❦ HENRIETTA POLYDORE, HENRIETTA MAYER POLYDORE, AND JANE E. MAYER

1   Gloucestershire to St. Louis (Spring 1854) [via rail Gloucestershire to Liverpool, ship/river boat to New Orleans and St. Louis]

2   St. Louis to Salt Lake City (Summer–Fall 1855) [via Oregon/Mormon Trails]

⚜ HENRIETTA MAYER POLYDORE

1   Salt Lake City to Gloucestershire (Spring 1856)
    [via Oregon/Mormon Trails to Florence, N.T., Missouri River
    to St. Louis, Miss. River boat to New Orleans, ship to Liverpool,
    train to Cheltenham]

2   Gloucestershire to New Orleans (Fall 1856, with parents/siblings)
    [via rail to Liverpool, ship to New Orleans]

3   New Orleans to Arkansas (early 1857, relocation with parents/
    siblings to cotton farm)
    [via Miss. River steamer]

4   Arkansas to New York to Arkansas (Fall 1858, with daughter
    Henrietta eastbound only)
    [via Miss. River steamer to St. Louis, rail to Greencastle,
    Washington, N.Y., and return]

5   Arkansas to Miss. City, Miss. (early 1866, relocation with parents/
    siblings to Barnes Hotel)
    [via Miss. River steamer]

6   Miss. City to Gloucestershire to Miss. City (1866)
    [via ship New Orleans to Liverpool, rail to Gloucestershire and
    return]

7   Miss. City to Louisiana (mid/late 1880s, relocation with mother/
    sibling post–Barnes Hotel) [via Miss. River steamer]

8   Louisiana to Utah (presumably Ogden/Salt Lake City) to
    Louisiana (1897) [via Miss. River boat or rail to St. Louis, rail to
    Utah and return]

9   Louisiana to Utah (early 1900s, relocation to live with brother in
    Ogden/Pleasant Grove) [via rail]

⚜ HENRIETTA POLYDORE AND JANE MAYER RICHARDS

1   Salt Lake City to St. Louis (Fall 1858, with infant Phineas H.
    Richards and Judge Eckels' entourage)
    [via Oregon/Mormon Trails to Ft. Leavenworth, Missouri River
    steamer to St. Louis]

❧ JANE MAYER RICHARDS

1   St. Louis to Arkansas (December 1858, with sister Henrietta
     Mayer Polydore) [via Miss. River steamer]
2   Arkansas to Salt Lake City (presumably 1865, post–Civil War,
     minus Phineas) [via Miss. River steamer to St. Louis, Missouri
     River steamer to Florence, N.T., Oregon/Mormon Trails]

❧ HENRIETTA POLYDORE

1   St. Louis to Gloucestershire (November 1858–January 1859, with
     Judge Eckels to Washington and with Royal Messenger thereafter
     to Liverpool) [via rail to Greencastle, Washington, and N.Y., ship
     to Liverpool, rail to Gloucestershire]
2–? Multiple trips between Gloucestershire and Miss. City (from 1866
     until death in Miss. in 1874)

❧ SAMUEL W. RICHARDS

1   Liverpool to Salt Lake City (Fall 1854) [via ship to Boston, rail to
     St. Louis (via Ontario), Missouri River steamer to Florence, N.T.,
     Oregon/Mormon Trails]
2   Salt Lake City to Liverpool (Fall 1857) [via Oregon/Mormon Trails
     to Florence, N.T., Missouri River steamer to St. Louis, rail to
     Philadelphia, N.Y., Boston, ship to Liverpool]
3   Liverpool to Salt Lake City/Provo (Winter–Spring 1858) [via ship
     to New Orleans, Miss. River steamer to St. Louis, Missouri River
     steamer to Florence, N.T., Oregon/Mormon Trails]

Index

(illustration references in italics)

Red River, 86n15

Republican Party: anti-polygamy stance of, 41

Reynolds, George, 72–73

Richard, John Baptiste, 95n39

Richards, Franklin D., 62, 65, 184

Richards, Helena L. Robinson, 59, 62

Richards, Jane Elizabeth Mayer, 34–35, 57, 62, 64, 65, 66, 67n28, 77, 90n25, 99, 119n21, 155, 179n11, 201, 203, 217; accompanies Henrietta Polydore to East, 139n10, 149, 151, 156–57, 176; death of, 180–81; defended by Hosea Stout, 108; joins extended family in Arkansas, 178; marries Samuel W. Richards, 59, 62, 185; poem dedicated to, 227–28; returns to Salt Lake City, 179–80, 184; rumors of disenchantment with Latter-day Saint Church, 135–36, 180; sails for New Orleans, 60–61; travels, list of, 230–31; tuberculosis affliction, 136n7, 173, 218. See also Moore, Jane

Richards, Mary Haskin Parker, 124–25

Richards, Phineas, 67, 149, 155, 176, 178, 230; death of, 180–81, 218

Richards, Samuel W., 17, 34, 57n18 (continuation), 61, 64, 65, 77, 79, 90n24–25, 91n27, 120, 125, 138n9, 139n10, 155, 156n8, 165, 172, 179n11, 180, 201, 215–16; correspondence with Jane and Henrietta, 66–67; death of, 165, 189; failed publishing venture, 187–88; later life, 184–89; pardoned by Buchanan, 109; president of British Mission,

59–62, 66–67, 150n1, 215–16; returns to England, 155, 185, 214; stands for election, 108; takes sixth wife, 178–79; tensions with Brigham Young, 184–89; travels, list of, 231. See also Peckham, Sam

Richards, Willard D., 59, 184

Robinson, Helena L. See Richards, Helena L. Robinson

Robison (Robinson), Lewis, 90

Rose Canyon, 141–42

Rossetti family, 14, 34, 57, 63, 64, 173–74, 177, 189–90, 204, 215

Rossetti, Christina Georgina, 21, 29, 58, 171, 173, 177, 182, 189–90, 212, 224; composes poem in honor of Henrietta Polydore, 171; writes re Henrietta's death, 174–75; selected poetry of, 225–26

Rossetti, Dante Gabriel, 29, 56n18, 58, 59, 60, 63, 175, 177, 182, 189–90; sketches by, 58, 63, 224

Rossetti, Gabriele, 57

Rossetti, William Michael, 56n18, 58, 60, 63, 171, 177, 182

Rozsa, John, 152n3

Rupe, Jim, 98n1

Russia, 217

Sacramento, Calif., 87

St. Albans, Hertfordshire. See Cheltenham, Gloucestershire, England

St. Charles River, 199

St. Helena Parish, La., 183

St. Joseph, Mo., 99, 104, 107

St. Louis Democrat (newspaper), 131

St. Louis, Mo., 92, 107, 176, 178, 182

About the Editors

WILLIAM P. MACKINNON, an independent historian residing in Montecito, Santa Barbara County, California, has written extensively about territorial Utah and the American West
since 1963. His articles, chapters, essays, and book reviews have
appeared in more than thirty journals, monographs, and ency-
clopedias. The Arthur H. Clark Co., imprint of the University
of Oklahoma Press, published the two, award-winning volumes
of his documentary history of the Utah War of 1857–58, *At
Sword's Point.* He is a Fellow and Honorary Life Member of the
Utah State Historical Society and member of the Utah Crossroads Chapter of the Oregon-California Trails Association.
MacKinnon has been presiding officer of such diverse organizations as the Mormon History Association, Santa Barbara Corral
of the Westerners, Yale Library Associates, and Children's Hospital of Michigan. In his parallel business career, he has been a
vice president of General Motors Corporation and is president
of MacKinnon Associates, a management consulting firm. He is
an alumnus or veteran of Yale College (B.A., Magna Cum Laude
and Phi Beta Kappa), the Harvard Graduate School of Business
Administration (M.B.A.), and U.S. Air Force. MacKinnon and
his wife Pat, also a native of New York State, have five children
and nine grandchildren.

KENNETH L. ALFORD is a professor of Church History and Doctrine at Brigham Young University. After serving almost 30 years on active duty in the United States Army, he retired as a colonel in 2008. While on active military duty, Ken served in numerous assignments, including the Pentagon, eight years teaching computer science at the United States Military Academy at West Point, and four years as department chair and professor teaching strategic leadership at the National Defense University in Washington, D.C. He has served as the Religious Education Teaching Fellow and is the current Ephraim Hatch Teaching and Learning Faculty Fellow at Brigham Young University. He is an Honorary Life Member of the Utah State Historical Society and member of the Utah Crossroads Chapter of the Oregon-California Trails Association. He is an alumnus of Brigham Young University (B.A., Magna Cum Laude, Highest Honors, Phi Kappa Phi, and Valedictorian, College of Social Sciences), the University of Southern California (M.A.), the University of Illinois at Urbana-Champaign (M.C.S.) and George Mason University (Ph.D.). His books include *Utah and the American Civil War: The Written Record*; *Saints at War: The Gulf War, Afghanistan, and Iraq*; *Civil War Saints*; and *Latter-day Saints in Washington, D.C.* Ken and his wife, Sherilee, have four children and eighteen grandchildren.